YOUR TOTAL IMAGE

YOUR TOTAL IMAGE

IMAGE

Philippa Davies

PIATKUS

To Dai

© 1990 Philippa Davies

First published in 1990 by
Judy Piatkus (Publishers) Ltd,
5 Windmill Street, London W1

Reprinted 1990
Paperback edition first published 1991

British Library Cataloguing in Publication Data

Davies, Philippa
    Your total image
    1. Man. Self-presentation
    I. Title
    302.5'4

ISBN 0–86188–842–1 (Hbk)
ISBN 0–7499–1025–9 (Pbk)

Designed by Paul Saunders
Cover design by Ken Leeder
Edited by Betty Palmer
Photography by Ron Sutherland
Typeset in 11/13 pt Lasercomp Sabon
Printed and bound in Great Britain by
Butler & Tanner Ltd, Frome, Somerset

CONTENTS

ACKNOWLEDGEMENTS

Special thanks
to Gill Cormode, Betty Palmer and Dasha Shenkman.
to Gary Thomas, Joan Thomas, Rees and Betty Davies.
to Sue Berry and Elaine Clerici.
to Lyn Harrell-Gentle, Sherry Maugé, Tom Karol and Chris Kelly for
modelling.
to Ghia and to Gregory Johnson for make-up and styling.

The author and publishers would like to thank Aquascutum and Jaeger
Man for providing the clothes for photography.

The photographs on page 10 are reproduced courtesy of Camera Press.

chapter one

INTRODUCTION: YOUR TOTAL IMAGE AND YOU

This book is for people who are good at something. You may be a professional with a thriving career, an entrepreneur with a growing business or someone who is returning to work, having successfully raised a family. You will have dedicated time and effort to becoming 'good at something'. Understandably, in doing so, you may have neglected a most important aspect of your self-promotion, the way in which you present yourself to others: YOUR TOTAL IMAGE.

Do the signals you send out reflect your abilities? Today, it is not enough simply to be 'good at something'; other people have to *see* that you are good at something. The signals you send out let other people know 'who you are'. You send these signals through many channels. The choices you make about your appearance, your posture and body language, your voice and speech, your surroundings and even the stationery you choose, convey powerful messages to others. The following chapters examine in detail how to make these signals work for you.

This book is about self-development. It is not about trying to be someone else, or behaving and representing yourself in ways that do not feel comfortable. All of us know or have met someone who attempts to represent themselves very differently from how we suspect they really are. Your total image succeeds when it is a true reflection of yourself, rather than an artificially imposed way of looking and speaking. My aim is to get you to ask yourself questions, rather than for me to supply glib answers.

YOUR TOTAL IMAGE is not about rights and wrongs. Nobody can objectively prescribe a 'correct' way to present yourself. Self-presentation is about interaction: about conveying the appropriate signals for the situation and the other people involved. Through understanding and awareness of these signals you can make yourself far more adaptable, both personally and professionally.

To these ends, YOUR TOTAL IMAGE starts 'inwards' and works 'outwards'. The second chapter looks at self-image and psychological orientation – why and how we choose to project signals. This is followed by a view on how others perceive us, and discusses how we can make an appropriate first impression. Then I look at what is seen, through body language and posture, clothing and grooming. I go on to consider what is heard in voice and speech, followed by a chapter on the signals you send when speaking in public. Chapter Eight concerns itself with the image you present at work; the signals you send during conversation, meetings, interviews and on the telephone. Finally, I consider messages that you send through your surroundings and 'accessories' such as office furnishings and even notepaper. As this is a wide-ranging subject, there is a reading list at the end, should you wish to take certain topics further.

You cannot prevent the signals conveyed by your total image being read by others. Everyone you meet for the first time will take a reading. When first impressions matter most, the signals are at their most potent. Many people are 'read', and they in turn read others, several times a day. Though there are times when we may wish it were otherwise, our appearance and behaviour constantly influence others. The more confidence and control we have over these signals, the lower our level of self-consciousness and the easier it becomes to fulfil our aims.

I try very hard not to judge others by the way they present themselves. As my job requires me to analyse these signals and in many cases to refine them, I try to separate the person from the impression. This is often very difficult. In my experience, many people do themselves and their abilities a great disservice through poor self-presentation. Yet happily, by making changes in two or three aspects of their presentation, they can succeed in dramatically improving the impression they create. Other people respond to them differently and, in turn, this makes them feel better about themselves. For example, someone who speaks abruptly, who favours a severe style in clothes and who usually moves rapidly, in an impatient manner will find that when they modify these qualities they become much more accessible to others.

Almost everyone can make some improvements in the way they present themselves. Many job advertisements these days demand 'excellent communication skills' and yet few people are trained in this area. In my work experience I have found top international management consultants as receptive and keen to improve as junior managers just starting out on their careers. Indeed, to inspire confidence and lead others, you *must* develop your presentation skills.

YOUR TOTAL IMAGE AND SOCIETY

It is three weeks before a general election. The ruling party are doing poorly in opinion polls, and the view of the electorate seems to be that those in power represent the minority interests of the wealthy and privileged. The party leader, who is normally immaculately dressed and coiffed, is given extensive media coverage while visiting a children's home and a large factory. She is shown wearing a casual overcoat and headscarf, chatting amiably with children and workers alike. Image 'adjustment' succeeds and her party's ratings soar. Her appearance, her behaviour and the setting in which she is seen have worked together to convey a convincing total image.

In politics, especially in America, image – the way others perceive you – is extremely important. In every presidential election but one this century (when Jimmy Carter won), the taller candidate has succeeded. In the 1988 election, Michael Dukakis's reluctance to wear shoulder pads to make himself look bigger was cited by the press as a contributory factor to the failure of the Democrats.

In Britain, Margaret Thatcher epitomises the successful politician who has built her image to help her win elections. Unlike the fussy bows and characterless dresses that she used to favour, she now wears a distinctive uniform of simple, elegant suits (see page 10). She has transformed her speaking voice dramatically; her pitch now sounds much lower and her pace is far more even. The image she presents is markedly more powerful than the one she had a few years ago. Her preoccupation with image is in marked contrast with politicians like Shirley Williams and Michael Foot.

Politicians have to pay great attention to image, because they rely on the media for exposure. In our society, the media are extremely powerful. And the media concern themselves primarily with image; how to represent people and events and how we, as readers, listeners and viewers perceive them. To become prominent in society and to establish a public profile we have to use the media.

For that reason, many companies now give their employees media training, on how to appear on television and speak to journalists. However, media training is pointless if the spokesperson has not considered self-presentation. The reputation and therefore profits of an organisation or company can undoubtedly be damaged or improved by the way its spokespersons present themselves to the media.

We, and the media, seek to define our society in terms of image. We show through the image we present where we see ourselves in society. I

9

Margaret Thatcher during her early days in office.

A more recent photograph, showing her new power look.

can opt to be a 'dinkie', a 'yuppie' or a 'thirtysomething' and have a greater sense of where I belong in society. I may choose to be none of these and yet simply by standing apart and knowing what I am not, I get a clearer picture of my place in the whole scheme of things.

At any given time, society has particular values and preoccupations. The image you project shows the extent to which you espouse these values. In the sixties, for instance, many people chose to rebel against the conservatism of the fifties. Outlandish clothes, cockney accents and laid-back behaviour indicated that you were part of an 'alternative' society. At the time of writing we are going through a period of shifting preoccupations; consumerism and materialism thrive alongside the growing concern for the environment and 'green' issues. It will be interesting to note how the way we present ourselves to one another will be affected by these value shifts.

Several months ago, a panel of body language experts were interviewed on television. They were asked how would society be affected if everyone knew and understood about body language. As with one voice, they replied that it would benefit enormously; we would be far more civilised and there would be far more understanding between people and a greater awareness of the needs of others. I hope our concern with the environment is matched by growing interest in how we interact with each other, as well as with the planet.

So, for you who are already 'good at something' I hope this book helps you present an adaptable total image that does justice to your abilities. In turn, I hope that you will achieve greater understanding of why others present themselves as they do.

chapter two

DISCOVERING YOUR IMAGE

Why is it that some people project themselves far better than others? Why do some people rapidly inspire confidence and trust when you meet them, while others make you feel ill-at-ease? What is the connection between how individuals see themselves and how they project their image to others?

You can improve the image you project only if you know who you are. If you have little appreciation of your strengths and weaknesses then you cannot possibly decide on areas for improvement. And this involves self-examination.

LOOKING AT YOURSELF

Presentation skills are threatening to some people because there is a strong connection between individual history and self-presentation. As someone who was constantly told as a child that you were ugly by being unfavourably compared with a good-looking brother or sister, you may avoid thinking about your appearance. Or as someone who was encouraged to talk a great deal and was often the centre of attention as a child, you may have grown up into an adult who talks a great deal, in a loud voice, and who likes to dominate conversation.

When we learn about ourselves, we have to look at our faults and our good points. This can involve a loss of 'face' and having to admit that we are all vulnerable. To some people, vulnerability is a dirty word. They would like to pretend that they have never known or experienced fear, that they are all-powerful and all-knowing. That is the aggressive, bluff image they present to the world. In denying vulnerability, being afraid to say 'I don't know' or 'I would like to learn' or 'I have areas of weakness', they view the world through blinkered eyes. Yet as children one of the ways we learn about and construct our view of the world is through fear. We learn that if we destroy another child's toy we are punished, so we become afraid to do it again. If a mother leaves a child for a period of time, the child will become frightened and insecure and worry that she may do so again. Early experiences of fear and vulnerability exert strong influences on the adults we become.

If you start to present yourself as a successful person, others will respond to you accordingly and your actions will have to support your image. Some of us are afraid to aim high, because nobody becomes successful without learning to deal with failure. It is often easier to stay as we are than to accept a challenge. Improving your total image is about accepting that challenge.

USING CRITICISM CONSTRUCTIVELY

We cannot develop ourselves without feedback from other people. Feedback is of course, a 'nicer' word for criticism. We are often so comfortable and familiar with the way we present ourselves that, unless we seek criticism from others or they volunteer it, we cannot see room for improvement.

Feedback from others serves to confirm for you that the image you present to the world is working. If you present yourself as a confident, successful individual and see that version accepted, then your self-image is reinforced. When others reject that version, and respond to you as though you are insecure and inadequate, your self-image may be shaken. Some people are very dependent on reinforcement from other people around them to maintain self-image. Other personalities may believe that anyone who disagrees with them or views the world very differently is a fool.

Giving and receiving feedback can be difficult. There is no point in criticising some aspect of a person that is not capable of change – there is no point in saying to someone who is short, 'What a shame you're not a lot taller.' There is, however, a point in suggesting that wearing one colour, rather than 'shortening' the body by wearing blocks of different colours, gives a more streamlined appearance. There is also a point in suggesting that standing and sitting in an upright manner, and using expansive rather than protective body language, makes a person appear more rather than less significant. When criticising others, comment on positive aspects and make realistic, constructive suggestions.

Inviting criticism from others requires courage. Many of us would prefer to carry on as we are, without the trauma of change. Choose someone you can trust, whom you know well and whom you can depend on to be generous about your interests. Explain to them that you wish to change an aspect of your presentation and that you would like their help and advice. Ask them to give you feedback and thank them when they do. Get the person who is giving you feedback to be as specific and detailed as possible, and if necessary seek a second opinion.

People often criticise without realising it. Compliments are a form of positive criticism and many of us feel uncomfortable giving and receiving them. In complimenting someone else, we suspect we may be being too personal, while we often accept compliments with embarrassment and ill-grace, saying 'oh, this old thing' when something we are wearing is admired or 'I'm not so sure' when we are congratulated on making a good impression on someone else. We could, instead, accept the compliment graciously, thanking the giver, and allowing ourselves a pat on the back.

There are some people who use compliments constantly as a way of ingratiating themselves with others and we suspect their motives. The most effective compliments are ones where you suspect the feedback is true, and are delighted to receive confirmation of it from another source.

People may unwittingly criticise your presentation skills. When others constantly ask you to repeat yourself, because they cannot understand your speech, they are criticising an aspect of your presentation. If a good friend says that she likes your hair longer, she is giving you feedback. Perhaps people are always telling you to cheer up, in which case you could choose to change your habitual posture or body language or facial expression. The more you investigate the feedback by asking for specific details – 'Do you think I talk too quickly or too quietly?' or 'Should I grow my hair again, do you think?' or 'Does my face look glum, or am I slumping?' – the more you can do something with it.

Sometimes criticism is wantonly destructive. Second-hand criticism of the 'so and so said ...' variety is unfair unless it is easy for you to verify it. Ask yourself what the motives are behind such criticism and choose whether to accept it or not. Remember, you can always ask if someone would like to be criticised: 'Would you like me to suggest something about your presentation?'; the other person can refuse.

Besides friends, colleagues and relatives you can use experts and your own resources to give you feedback. There is an army of specialists available to help you improve your presentation and communication.

When possible, use personal recommendation to choose among them. Video equipment, mirrors, tape recorders and the response you get from others also help you monitor your progress.

Exercise

Your self-image is created by an assessment of your strengths and weaknesses. To do this takes a certain amount of courage. It can be useful to describe yourself in terms of strengths and weaknesses as two or three other significant people in your life see you, and then to describe how you see yourself. You may find the exercise indicates that you see yourself very differently from others, and the image you project needs attention; or that you have no idea how others see you, in which case you could do with some criticism; or that you are seeing yourself in a very poor light, in which case you need to boost your self-image and to seek constructive help and feedback from others.

YOUR SELF-IMAGE

The image you present to the outside world will often be regarded by others as a reflection of your level of self-esteem. We describe people as 'taking a pride in themselves', 'liking the sound of their own voice', 'appearing very self-possessed'. To take an interest in your self-development, whether in terms of seeking insight into your personal psychology or refining your presentation, indicates that you already have a certain level of self-regard. You believe that 'you' are of value and have potential to grow and change.

To present yourself well, you must appreciate your good points and understand your weaknesses. What you may perceive as a weakness need not necessarily be so; when two shy people meet, their shyness for a moment helps them to establish empathy. The way we present ourselves in life is indirect. We cannot tell others exactly what we think of them, or exactly what we want; we have to consider the needs of others, and how we preserve a civilised level of behaviour. When we are confident about our good points we can highlight them.

You may be fat, and embarrassed by your size. But the fat person who accepts his or her physique and is fit and healthy, who dresses in an attractive way and who realises that he or she loves communicating with others and makes them respond and so polishes those skills, will present an attractive self-image. Realising that you are always trying to impose your views on others, you may choose to make your distinctive appearance less so, and learn to listen and encourage others to speak. You may still enjoy the skill of maintaining the floor very effectively. If you feel completely inadequate in social situations, you may realise that other people are shy too and that you are a good listener. You may notice that if you wear an interesting tie or brooch, it usually causes comments from other people and then a conversation can start. You may realise that your sense of humour is an asset, and start actively to seek out people who look as though they share the same trait.

Your self-image is subject to all sorts of influences, your parents and upbringing being among the most important. The parent defines the child to a large extent, teaches the child who he or she is. Perhaps your parents did not appreciate your achievements when you were a child and gave you little praise. In that case you may well have a tendency to be excessively self-critical, and find it difficult to give yourself that pat on the back that we all need. Maybe you are always setting yourself impossibly high standards and constantly failing to reach them. When others criticise you, you may react with too much sensitivity. In turn, you may also set very high standards for others and be all too ready to criticise them ...

Think about adjusting your standards for yourself and others to a realistic level and take time out for activities (going for a stroll, listening to music, playing with children or animals) that are not goal-orientated.

Self-image is also influenced by experience. Many people who have had *one* bad experience when addressing an audience, view themselves as 'hopeless at public speaking'. If other people reinforced this view at the time of the event, then they strengthen your self-censure. If you are constantly learning from experience that you are not valued and others respond to you accordingly, then unless you have a stored sense of your worth and achievements your self-esteem may plummet.

If your self-esteem is very low, then improving your 'outer' image will be of limited benefit. The problem needs tackling from the inside with a professional counsellor, psychotherapist or psychoanalyst.

Your self-regard can be boosted by working on your total presentation. For example, if you learn how to control nervousness when speaking in public, then others will perceive you as confident and react to you accordingly. Your audience will look forward to what you have to say. If you look as though you care for your appearance, we take that to indicate that you respect and value yourself as an individual and therefore have the capacity to respect and value others.

IDENTIFICATION AND INDIVIDUALITY

Human beings need *involvement and identification with other human beings*, but we also need *to assert our individuality*. All of us have these two needs and sometimes they clash, causing conflict in ourselves and with others. Our whole existence revolves around these needs. When you were a small child, you wanted and needed your mother, but you also strove to break away from her and become independent. To my mind, these two basic needs are enormous influences on how we present ourselves to and interact with others.

Involvement and Identification with Others

You can show that you wish to be involved and identified with others through:

- your appearance – your clothes can show that you wish to fit in with a certain group of people, that you are a member of a particular tribe, be it yuppie or zulu.

- your posture and body language – watch a gang of fourteen-year-old boys and notice how they all swagger in a similar style as they walk along the road.

- the way you speak – to what extent do you adapt your speech and accent according to whom you are with? Some people are so keen to be accepted that they are always shifting accents so that they fit in with others.

- your language – the same gang of teenage boys may all swear loudly, using similar words to indicate membership of the gang and solidarity.

- your accessories – status symbols such as old schoolties, portable telephones, Citroën 2CVs indicate affiliation with certain groups in society.

- your surroundings – the latest in interior design in your home or office could demonstrate that you identify yourself with a select group of fashion leaders.

Establishing Individuality

But because all of us are a mixture of these two conflicting needs, these features of your total image can also indicate a desire to establish and assert your individuality by:

- your appearance – outrageous clothes and an unconventional haircut will set you apart from others, especially if you work in a sober traditional business.

- posture and body language – you may imitate Marilyn Monroe when you walk, setting yourself apart from other pedestrians. In a situation where you disagree with everyone else your body language may well show that you think differently from the rest of the group.

- your voice and speech – you may strengthen your accent in certain groups to assert your individuality. You may make your presence felt in public places like libraries and restaurants by talking much louder than everyone else.

- your language – you may use complicated language to establish your superiority over others.

- your accessories – these can reflect your achievements and provide evidence of your social and financial standing: clusters of diamonds, hand-printed scarves, antique fob watches.

- your surroundings – may express your individuality through interesting works of art, unusual furniture.

From the above descriptions you may well gather that the success you may have in indicating involvement and/or establishing your individuality depends on the situation and the other people that you are with. A Rolex (known as a 'badge' by some professions), for instance, may show solidarity with the values of a group of top-earning salesmen and you could expect others in the group to be sporting 'badges'. The same watch worn to a meeting of Friends of the Earth would certainly set you apart and might even cause some raised eyebrows and speculation about your priorities.

Other qualities connect to these two fundamental needs. The extent to which *you seek approval and acceptance from others, wish to conform* and *adapt to the needs of others* links to the need for involvement and identification. If in a particular situation you are most concerned with asserting your individuality, then goals like *distinguishing yourself, emphasising your achievements* and showing that *you have your own strong opinions* may come to the fore. And we cannot compartmentalise these needs. You may want to win approval from another person and involve yourself with them through emphasising your achievements and thereby establishing your individuality.

Much of what we do and how we present ourselves depends upon a delicate balancing act of the two needs. The man or woman who agrees with everyone all the time, listens attentively and rarely ventures a personal opinion is *presenting an image* of someone who is strongly motivated by the need for involvement (I say 'presenting an image' because we do not know what is going on inside his or her head), while the speaker who constantly challenges others and dominates conversation with strong opinions and little fear of offending others is presenting a contrasting image of someone who is strongly motivated to demonstrate individuality.

EXTROVERTS AND INTROVERTS

Your image of yourself is also influenced by the levels of extroversion or introversion in your personality. People do not fall neatly into one category or the other. Someone who is an outgoing, friendly, expressive extrovert much of the time may also have an introverted side, at certain times and in certain situations. A quiet, thoughtful, contained introvert may have developed extrovert skills to cope with certain demands of life. Most people are a mixture, though one tendency will usually dominate.

Extroverts have a strong 'outer reality'. That is to say they enjoy being in company and communicating with others a great deal, prefer action to contemplation, are keen to be liked and to fit in with others. The extrovert's self-image is likely to include an appreciation of his or her 'people-skills'.

Introverts have a strong 'inner reality'. That is to say they are quite happy to spend time alone examining their own minds, when they form strong opinions and set clear goals for themselves. The introvert's self-image is likely to include an appreciation of his or her 'independent ideas'.

Extroverts, then, on the whole have a greater need for involvement and identification with others, while introverts have a need to establish their independence. Extroverts may well avoid self-analysis and feel uncomfortable spending a great deal of time on their own. Introverts may well avoid situations like public speaking and feel uncomfortable when they have to socialise a great deal.

How does extroversion and introversion affect your total image? Dorothy Rowe, in her fascinating study of these different orientations

19

The Successful Self, explains how introverts and extroverts have different styles of doing things and presenting themselves (see Chapter Five for a comment from her on appearance). She explains that extroverts seek greater stimulation from others, while introverts avoid the risk of over-stimulation from other people.

An extrovert may seek to stimulate other people to get them to respond and to obtain greater involvement, through:

- using a lot of expressive, expansive body language.

- wearing bright colours, clothes that cause a reaction from others, creating a friendly appearance that they think others will like.

- talking a great deal to get people's attention, or being afraid to talk in case of incurring disapproval from others.

- speaking a lot, in an excited manner to keep others stimulated, giving other people a lot of attention, using a lot of facial expression, asking others lots of questions to get them involved.

- dramatising descriptions when talking.

- filling their surroundings with lots of stimulating clutter and artefacts, making the place look 'friendly' with plants and flowers, pictures of family and friends.

An introvert may avoid stimulation and be preoccupied with personal achievement and ideas rather than people. He or she may indicate this through:

- using contained body language and not seeking to stimulate others or dramatise messages through the use of body language.

- wearing clothes that do not stimulate a reaction from others, plain colours and simple shapes. Appearance could express individuality, lack of concern for the approval of others, or exclusivity and therefore seeking admiration from a select few.

- not finding it necessary to talk because the need for involvement with others is not a priority; or talking a great deal to express ideas.

- speaking quietly and taking time to think while talking; being specific, precise and accurate about certain details, choosing words carefully.

- expressing definite views and opinions and not actively seeking responses from others. Being more interested in ideas than feelings.

- not worrying about surroundings; thriving in chaos (Dorothy Rowe points out that introverts can tolerate a lot of external chaos, as long as their 'inner reality' is in order); not appearing to care what other people think. Or choosing stark and minimalist surroundings that reflect distinction and individuality, free of excess stimulation.

Each one of us constructs our own version of reality. To develop we need to appreciate this and to realise that the realities of others may be very different from our own. As an extrovert you may wish to expand your sense of your 'inner life' by taking time out to do quiet, thoughtful activities in solitude. An introvert who senses limitations may wish to work on 'people skills' – on focusing out and getting more involved with others.

Exercise

- To what extent are you introvert or extrovert? Is your self-presentation working against this? Work out your attitude towards spending a lot of time alone and time spent with numbers of other people. What do you find most demanding – solitude or socialising? Are you trying to be more extrovert or introvert than you really are?

ROLE-PLAYING AND LABELS

In our lives we play a number of roles and present different images of ourselves according to whom we are with. The man who is a tyrannical lion in the office may well play the role of a timid mouse at home with his wife.

In your self-presentation you attach labels to yourself that indicate these roles. Sometimes these labels can limit your adaptability. The woman who always speaks in a breathy, little-girl voice may find difficulties influencing others in her managerial position at work. The man who always wears a uniform of smart pin-striped suit and striped shirt may fail to reassure his unhappy teenage son that he can begin to understand his problems.

The roles we adopt are often to do with responsibility. Some people are constantly taking on more than they can cope with, in order to please others. Others like to play at being leader because it reinforces their sense of independence and individuality. And for the opposite reasons you may shun responsibility. Perhaps you do not want to assert your authority because it means that you stand apart from others and may offend them.

Or maybe you avoid responsibility because you do not want to be the same as everybody else: you are a free spirit, an independent, free-thinking individual.

Your total image should reflect these roles and how effectively you play them. Some of the roles are dictated at birth – your race, sex, age, your physical characteristics, and your place in the family. Other roles will have been created as you have progressed socially and professionally. You will have certain roles that have obvious names, such as your job title – personnel director, teacher, writer – and your hobbies will provide a further description – footballer, reader, television fan. If you live with others you will have a role within that structure – mother, dependent, breadwinner, lover, husband.

To these roles we need to bring certain qualities. The manager may need to have leadership skills, consideration for others, the ability to inspire those under his or her guidance. The footballer must be able to work in a team, be competitive and be physically fit.

We label ourselves on the inside too. Earlier on, when talking about criticism, I described a common tendency – that of being highly self-critical. Our inner voices will have recorded other messages and many of them will have been 'taped' from our parents as we grew up. These messages are often statements that describe us, such as 'you're lazy', 'you're attractive', or commands and rules: 'you must work hard', 'never talk to strangers', 'life is a miserable uphill struggle'. Because we heard these frequently, and in our formative years, they usually stick. Some of them have a direct bearing on the image we present to the world. It is hardly remarkable that someone who has been repeatedly labelled as 'too fat, you really must lose weight' habitually uses body language which conceals and apologises for their body. Someone who has been told repeatedly 'be quiet, you're getting on my nerves' may find it difficult and awkward to make conversation with strangers.

Exercises

- What roles do you play? In terms of work, the family and leisure time? Is there a balance between taking responsibility and team effort? How would you describe the qualities you demonstrate in those roles? Are you getting sufficiently involved with others but also being able to express your individuality and achieve goals?

- What labels and messages do you constantly give yourself? Are you constantly saying 'I'm to blame', or 'I'll take responsibility for everything', or 'I'll do it because I'm keen to please', or 'I'm right and I'll change everyone else's mind'? Check these and realise that they can be changed, by being replaced with different affirmations: 'I can't do everything', 'I need time for myself', 'you have your view and I can respect your opinion, even though it is different from mine.'

YOUR BODY IMAGE

The mind and the body are very closely connected and interdependent. In the past they have been regarded as separate entities; nowadays physical therapies are prescribed for stress, depression and anxiety, while counselling and various forms of therapy can help those suffering from AIDS, cancer or obesity.

Having a good body image is an important part of self-esteem. This is not the same as having a good body. It is all too easy to overstretch the body at the expense of the mind and vice versa. Top athletes can become obsessive and vulnerable in their desire to win, to the point that they abuse their bodies by taking drugs such as anabolic steroids. Executives spend long hours overloading their minds with problems at work and take themselves to the point of physical collapse. In both instances, mind and body have become disconnected; the athlete viewing the body as a machine rather than a part of the whole self, the executive concentrating on the mind at the expense of the body.

A good body image is all to do with a balanced integration between mind and body. You may have a poor body image and yet your actual body may well represent the ideal shape as dictated by our society. Even those whom many of us would regard as being near to physical 'perfection', athletes and dancers, may have problems with body image. When the body becomes the means of earning a living, or a means of asserting superiority over others, or something that has to be rigidly controlled, then the mind–body balance can be disturbed. The mind may become obsessive about pushing the body to its limits, developing the body into a perfect ideal or constantly punishing the body through strict dieting and over-rigorous regimes. In some people, a 'divorce' between mind and body results in eating disorders, denial of feelings in the mind being expressed instead through the body. Obsessive physical habits can become the outward manifestation of inner inadequacies.

Society puts pressures on us to conform in terms of body image. The media are fixated with bodies and both advertisements and news items are full of the current physical ideal, lithe muscular young men and women

23

displaying their honed torsos in skimming lycra. In terms of body image, too, we have the need to *identify with others* and to *make ourselves stand out*: we may want to conform to a physical ideal or to be admired by others for our bodies. People who do not conform to society's current ideals of height and slenderness may be stared at in the street.

Your body image is also linked to your sexuality. You may have sexual difficulties if you think your body is ugly, disgusting or shameful. If you regard your body as a machine, you may think of sex as a mechanical process where emotion has no place. Excessive concern with a physical ideal may mean that you have unrealistically high expectations of sex. Perhaps you habitually use your body to dominate or submit to others.

And of course we express our sexuality in our self-presentation. Some people seem to have a strong drive to display their sexuality, through alluring clothes, a macho strut or Monroe-like wiggle, flirtatious eye contact or pouting mouth. Others are far more low-key about appearing 'sexual', following the dictum that 'the most important sexual organ is the brain'. We can put on or lose weight so that we deny or disguise our sexuality.

Body image can reflect your perception of your significance and standing compared with others. When we consider someone unimportant we describe them as a 'nobody'. We regard body image stereotypically; large people are powerful, threatening, significant, can take a lot of responsibility and, if female, may appear especially maternal. Small people may compensate for their lack of stature by behaving in a self-important way (the Napoleon syndrome) or may use their 'smallness' to avoid responsibility, letting larger people assume a parental role. Size is also linked to control and power; obsessive dieting gives the confused and powerless an opportunity to exert rigid control over *something*, the size of their body, while uncontrolled eating may be a comfort to those who are over-controlled in other areas of their lives.

If you feel uncomfortable or critical of your body it will affect your total image. Your body is, after all, what others see. Under scrutiny from others you will feel ill-at-ease. With a positive body image, accepting your body as it is, tuning in to its signals and caring for it, your total image will benefit:

- posture and body language – we can use posture and body language to persuade others that we are larger or smaller than we are, to look apologetic for our presence and even to hide parts that we do not like (by sitting with arms crossed over the stomach for instance). If you like your body you will look as though you are of 'some standing'.

- your appearance – with a poor attitude towards the body, it is easy to pretend that 'clothes don't matter', and dodge the need to come to terms with it. With a balanced appreciation of your body image, you can dress so as to play up your good points and play down the bad ones.

- your voice – if you habitually adopt poor posture and ignore signals of tension and stored emotions in the body (see Chapter Four) then voice production, which depends on the efficient use of the body, may suffer.

IMPROVING BODY IMAGE

To improve body image, you need to work on mind and body. Exercise can help stress, because it produces endorphins in the body, which help combat stress reactions. Other physical therapies like massage and aromatherapy can help you relax; for these you have to stop playing the role of 'driver' and put yourself in the 'passenger' seat. That shift of responsibility alone can help you relax.

Here are some further suggestions to consider:

- If we believe that as human beings we have potential for personal growth and development, we need to work on minds and bodies. You may have a fit, healthy body that is regularly exercised and yet your body image could be poor. Explore and stimulate your mind, too. Learn a new skill, read more and extend your areas of interest, join an evening class or group activity relating to the mind. Some physical activities, like certain martial arts and yoga, have a 'cerebral' side that can be explored.

- If you have relegated body image to a low priority, then it may be time to start giving it more attention. The temptation is to rush in with a punishing exercise schedule and then lose heart because of trying to achieve too much. Stretch yourself – gradually. If you are very unfit, begin with a brisk daily walk. Consult an expert to assess your fitness and work out a progressive programme. Give yourself physical 'treats' such as massage, aromatherapy, relaxation techniques (see Chapter Four), shiatsu massage (Chinese method based on principles of acupuncture), reflexology (foot massage).

- Choose body work that suits your personality and provides a balance with other areas of your life. If you spend a lot of time alone, then group exercise like aerobics classes or playing team games will provide different stimulation. If you are surrounded by others most of the time, then exercise like swimming or running will give you an opportunity to think without distraction. Exercise needs to suit your lifestyle; if you travel a great deal, something like running or following an exercise video, which you can do in most places, will be easier to maintain. 'Larks' who rise early and do their best work in the morning may want to exercise in the afternoon or evening; 'owls' who are at their best later on in the day may be better off exercising in the morning.

- balance 'being' and 'doing'. If your working life is not very challenging and you spend a lot of time serving others, set yourself some goals in your exercise. If you are very goal-orientated at work, then find a physical activity that you can enjoy without needing to achieve goals all the time.

- be realistic about your diet. Don't be obsessive about food and constantly feel that you are denying yourself. If you eat out a great deal, a few simple guidelines like always drinking mineral water with wine, avoiding puddings and not drinking too much coffee, especially late at night, are easy to follow. For some people, a dietary obsession becomes the major goal of their lives; this must be at the expense of other considerations (moral and spiritual self-examination for instance) and they become diet bores.

- accept your body image as something that establishes your individuality. That's not to say that if you are overweight and it is affecting your health you should not do something about it. Treat your body with respect, caring for and maintaining, it and learn to use posture, body language and clothes to your advantage. Enjoy your 'distinctiveness'.

- workaholics only function efficiently for a certain number of hours. Better to do efficient mental work for seven hours, then take some time to do some physical activity, than to work inefficiently for ten hours. The exercise will help you build energy. If you improve your body image, you are likely to feel a lot more confident in interviews, meetings and presentations – anywhere, in fact, where others are putting you under scrutiny.

chapter three

THE FIRST IMPRESSION

The image you project is only effective if other people accept it. If you send out a set of signals, and they are constantly misinterpreted by others you will feel misunderstood.

There are three parts to presenting an image:

- *your self-image.*

- *your projected image* – the way in which you think the world sees you. The closer this representation is to your self-image, the better and the more secure you can feel about it.

- *your received image* – the way in which others *really* see you. If this is at odds with your projected image, it may be because you have not spared the time and effort to consider how you are presenting yourself.

In Chapter Two, we considered your self-image. In this chapter, we shall move 'outwards' to consider the way you project your image and how others are receiving those signals.

PROJECTING YOURSELF

People often say to me: 'I'm always being told that I look sullen/bossy/supercilious/disorganised, but that's not the way I am at all. What can I do?' I usually suggest that they ask themselves the following questions.

Am I always comparing myself with others?

If you are highly self-critical and do not value your individuality it can make you too ready to compare yourself unfavourably with others. Failing to appreciate your achievements and good points, you'll always feel inadequate by comparison. Yet we can appreciate others without needing to be like them. Change your inner monologue. For instance, 'She looks much better than I do' can translate to: 'She looks lovely and the style suits her. I look very different from her and I too have made the best of myself.' Or 'He made a marvellous speech – I could never make one as well' to 'He made a marvellous speech and I can learn from it. My style and content would be different, though.' To an extent we have to compare ourselves with others to have some yardstick for our achievements, but being too competitive with insufficient appreciation of your own worth is destructive.

Am I trying too hard to assert my individuality?

You can be so desperate to establish an image that you fail to consider the reactions or needs of others. You may constantly try to shock others by demanding attention and being controversial and this behaviour can be an imposition – even offensive. Self-possessed people do not need to try that hard. They are not threatened by others and have no urge to overpower them. There is room for others to express their individuality, too, a sense of give and take. So 'I'm going to dominate this conversation to show how strong I am' can change to 'I will hear others out and consider what they say, before I make my point.' Or 'I am going to put posters up all over the office walls to cheer us up' can change to 'I'll put a poster in my corner of the office to cheer me up.'

Am I presenting myself as a stereotype?

As we are inundated with stereotypes in the media, it is hardly surprising that some of us should choose to model ourselves on them. Rather than considering our own strengths and weaknesses through self-examination, we adopt a ready-made image. And again, we can do this to fulfil our desires to identify and join with others or to indicate individuality. Teenagers, for instance, express identification with pop heroes through dressing like them. As we get older, the Next and Conran empires provide us with all we need for a yuppie image and lifestyle, and make it easy to be identified as a member of a certain section in society. We may, of course, choose to copy a more distinctive stereotype that makes us stand out. If you choose to model your image on a fifties glamour queen or an Edwardian huntin', shootin' and fishin' country gent, then you will make yourself distinctive and prominent.

Presenting yourself as a stereotype can be very restricting. Others may respond to you stereotypically – they may not see past the peroxide hair and provocative wiggle or deerstalker hat and upper-crust accent. They may mistrust your obvious 'disguise' and feel that you are not genuine. In show-business, of course, these 'larger than life' images can help people to rise to prominence.

Am I presenting myself in an out-of-date way?

Old habits die hard, and it is easy to take aspects of your image for granted. Perhaps you are still dressing as you did ten years ago, or being 'laid-back' like everyone was in the sixties. We seem to develop habits at various times in our lives that stay with us, even though our self-image may have changed. As a girl in your teens, you may have become self-conscious about developing breasts, and rounded your shoulders to make them less prominent. As a boy at puberty, you may have reacted to your voice becoming unreliable by developing the habit of mumbling. Unless you have made a conscious effort to counter these habits they may well persist into adulthood.

Am I failing to consider my total image?

When an individual sends out conflicting signals, others get confused. You may be immaculately groomed, but if you open your mouth and speak in a slovenly drawl the illusion will be ruined and others will sense inconsistency. Your appearance, behaviour and environment need to reinforce your efficiency, creativity or concern for others – whatever the qualities are that you wish to project – consistently.

THE FIRST IMPRESSION

When you first meet another person, you form a strong impression of them within the first few moments and a lasting opinion of them during the first thirty seconds to four minutes of meeting. First impressions are powerful and permanent.

We know that 'you shouldn't judge a book by its cover', but we persist in doing so. Why is this? Rationally, we should realise that the way someone presents themselves, their projected image, may not do justice to their true qualities. Yet we persist in making these instant judgements on one another.

We have to take decisions about others when we meet them to know how *to start and continue communication*. For instance, if you met me, and you attempted to stay impression-free then you would not know how to proceed in communication. You would not notice my clothes and hair. You would not notice that I was female. You would not notice that I was thirtysomething. You would not notice that I was five foot three with Celtic colouring. You would not notice what mood was indicated through my posture, body language and face. You might make the assumption that I spoke English, because we were in England. That is the sole guidance you would have on how to approach me.

Although most of us know someone who does seem almost this oblivious to others, it is clear that we cannot stop receiving impressions of others while our senses are operating. These impressions determine the way in which we respond to the other person.

At this hypothetical meeting between you and me, you will form a further set of impressions when I start to talk. You may notice that I am facially expressive when I speak. You may notice that I have a low-pitched voice with a Welsh accent. You may notice that I talk quickly and that I nod and smile quite a lot when I listen to you. You may notice that I appear to like talking a great deal . . .

You will probably have noticed quite a few other details. Depending on your preoccupations, you may have noticed my earrings, my teeth, my perfume, my hairstyle, my use of eye contact and the blouse I'm wearing. You may well have noticed how keen I seem to be to get involved with conversation and how interested I am in you.

When you meet me, you may:

- seek involvement, and identification with me.

- assert your individuality.

- seek to assess my individuality.

Again those two conflicting instincts, to join with others but also to establish your 'separateness', come into play. And your personality will influence which instinct prevails.

Let's look at how these needs can play their part in forming a first impression.

Seeking involvement with me

You may form an instant impression from my facial expression that I look friendly and approachable. You may decide that I appear to be the same age as you. You may, from the myriad of signals that I send off, decide that you just 'like the look of me' and sense that *we might have some things in common.*

Asserting your individuality

As you form your impression of me, you may decide that I look accessible/threatening/lively/timid and you will react accordingly. You may choose to respond by appearing receptive, respectful or bored. You may decide that we have *some apparently contrasting values*; maybe I am very well dressed, while you are less so. Perhaps you are well-spoken and fluent, while I am inarticulate and my speech is indistinct.

You may establish differences between you and me through contrasting behaviour, positioning yourself so that you look very different from how I look. If I am indicating nervousness through rapid eye contact, fidgety movements and hunched posture, you may give the impression of being relaxed, using an open gaze with a slight smile, and expansive body language with little distracting movement. You may use a different conversational style (see 'Meeting New People' later in this chapter): if I am talking quickly and with animation, you may heighten the differences between us by slowing down your speed and being more laid back.

Assessing my individuality

When you form your impression of me you will want to know what *qualities I have that you can respect or admire.* You will assess *in what ways I am like you and in what ways I am different.* If the ways in which I am different are ones that you can admire, so much the better. Maybe my Welsh accent is pleasing to your ear, and you think my posture and body language indicate confidence and self-esteem. Perhaps you think my clothes are well-chosen and that my face has an intelligent expression. I'd hope so, anyway....

We are rarely aware of these influences when we form impressions of one another and they often work simultaneously.

Each one of us has a system of values and beliefs which come into play when we form a first impression of another person. When those values

31

and beliefs are irrational and extreme, we become prejudiced. The order in which we notice characteristics of another person is as follows:

- colouring
- gender
- age
- size
- facial expression

- eye contact
- hair
- build
- clothes
- movement

Clearly, if a person is racially or sexually prejudiced, then their irrational attitudes will affect a meeting from the outset. They will notice immediately that the other person is of a race or sex that they are afraid of (because prejudice develops from fear and ignorance) and be blind to qualities that could temper that fear. Sometimes, of course, the prejudice may be milder, towards an accent perhaps or towards a facial expression. It may still succeed in 'putting you off' someone in the first few minutes of meeting them.

Reacting with prejudice is an example of 'reverse halo effect'. Many of us seem to want to believe in angels. When we meet someone for the first time we look for instant evidence, in the impression they make, that we like or dislike them. If we decide to approve, then most of what the other person does and says will seem to reinforce our initial favourable impression. We want to be right. We want to see the other person with a 'halo'. The world is easier to deal with and define if there are 'good guys' and 'bad guys'.

And the bad guys are surrounded by the 'reverse halo'. When we meet them and they look scruffy, or have bad teeth, or indicate through posture and body language that they can't be bothered to talk to us, then we dismiss them. Everything they say and do from then on adds further evidence of their being a bad lot. Something remarkable will have to happen to make us change our minds.

If you form a bad first impression of someone, then hear contradictory opinions which are highly favourable from a respected friend, do you really change your mind? I suspect that at best, most of us decide to 'take a second look'. For people like interviewers, the 'halo effect' can be a dangerous trap that can mar effective judgement.

PEOPLE LIKE US

We like 'people like us'. Unless we wish to isolate ourselves, we seek to involve ourselves with other people and find shared values and experiences. If we do not find some common area of understanding, then the relationship will progress no further.

So, when you *make a first impression* how does the 'people like us' factor affect you? The other person will respond with certain attitudes towards your race, age and gender and you may have to combat prejudice towards these. Concentrating on improving other aspects of your self-presentation may go some way to counteracting the negative stereotyping that still unfortunately persists. You can make yourself look younger or older, through hair-style, make-up, clothing, posture and energy of movement. You may even decide to ward off ageing through plastic surgery.

As a young person making a first impression on somebody a lot older, you need to consider that the other person may feel avuncular, patronising or in awe of your youth. To convey that you are responsible and work the 'people like us' factor, you could dress conservatively, take your time when you speak and avoid nervous mannerisms like giggling. Long hair on women looks less 'girlish' when it is put up.

As an older person making a first impression on someone a lot younger, you need to consider that the other person may feel respectful, rebellious or that you are 'out of touch'. You may wish to choose stylish clothes and a hair-style that shows awareness of current trends without slavishly following them. If you avoid slumping, maintain your body so that it is trim and you have sufficient physical energy and speak with clarity and pace, the 'people like us' factor should help you make a good first impression.

Avoid extremes. A twenty-year-old dressing and behaving as a forty-year-old seems incongruous; a forty-year-old does not want to be labelled 'mutton dressed as lamb'. Today, age is no longer the barrier it used to be.

When you consider the 'people like us' factor and gender, it is not surprising that at social events people of the same sex often huddle together. At work, as a woman making her first impression on a man, if you dress in flounces and frills, wear lots of make-up, speak in a high-pitched, breathy voice, smile a great deal and use a lot of protective body language you will emphasise your 'distinctiveness' from the man. You will have limited benefit from the 'people like us' factor. If as a man making a first impression on a woman you are heavily bearded, dressed in a severe way with padded shoulders that emphasise your muscular frame, talk in a very deep-pitched voice and use little expression, then again you'll accrue little benefit from the 'people like us' factor. Of course, that's not too say that you may not find the other person devastatingly sexually attractive...

Later in this chapter there is further consideration of the different presentation styles of men and women.

How you use your size and appearance can help build 'people like us' rapport. If you are very small, then you can use clothing, posture and body language, and positioning to make yourself appear larger. When you stand very close to a large person, your diminutive size is emphasised. A larger person has the reverse problem. He or she can seem threatening and dominating to small people. Adjusting body language and sitting whenever possible may help. You may be entirely different physically from another person, but you can still indicate common understanding through clothing and accessories. Many of us spend a lot of time and effort on our appearance, but give insufficient attention to how we can use clothing signals to show rapport with others. More about this in Chapter Five.

Occasionally you may want to make a good first impression and come up against impenetrable prejudice from the other person, that you can do nothing to change. This can be incredibly frustrating especially when the person is in a position of power. Take some consolation from the consideration that were you to enter some sort of relationship with this person, their fear of you would always be an issue.

We like 'people like us' when we share similar values and behaviour. This common ground may be obvious: you may be attracted to someone who looks like you. Less consciously, you may be attracted to someone for reasons that you cannot specify, and find out later, when you get to know them, that you have much in common in terms of family background and experience.

At a party, if you are wearing accessories that flaunt your wealth and indicate your regard for material possessions, you are more likely to attract the other Armani-suited Rolex-wearing guests than the guest in the kaftan with the CND badges. They will have spotted a 'person like them'. As a young newcomer to a company, looking nervous and insecure at the annual dinner, you may well be approached by another new recruit seeking solidarity. Through first impressions, you will have demonstrated similar attitudes to the situation.

Too much similarity, however, can make the 'people like us' factor into a problem. Turning up to an interview wearing an identical suit to the interviewer could cause embarrassment and a blurring of the distinction between your role and his or hers. If someone is wearing exactly the same outfit as you at a party, it could detract from your individuality and you may be tempted to go home and change. In the same way, it can be irritating to be introduced to someone just because they have the same distinctive accent as you do; you may feel patronised and that your individuality is being compromised. Why should someone assume that because you sound the same, you will have a lot in common? 'Joanne, you must meet Katie – she's from the States, too.' Although Joanne has lived in England for fifteen years, other people assume that she must want to meet other Americans. In fact she positively relishes her 'distinctiveness' and has no wish whatsoever to compromise it by being in the company of fellow Americans.

BEHAVIOUR BREEDS BEHAVIOUR

At a meeting you may spot Mike, who on first impression looks enthusiastic and expressive. As you consider yourself to have these qualities, and value them, Mike will attract you; he looks like a 'person like you'. If he's too much like you, however, both of you may start to assert your individuality and end up in competition. However, for the moment it looks as though you and Mike could have a fine time together, both being enthusiastic and expressive. Your behaviour could encourage Mike's behaviour and indicate approval of it, and vice versa.

Behaviour is highly contagious. Few of us have spent a couple of hours with a friend who is in a bad temper and not experienced a lowering of our mood. On first meeting someone who is obviously tense and edgy it is difficult not to assimilate some of these sensations yourself. In particular, our non-verbal behaviour posture, body language, eye contact, facial expression and sound of voice influence others.

Albert Mehrabian, a psychologist, has suggested that:

55% of the impression we make on others is determined by what they SEE. This includes colouring, appearance, posture, body language, facial expression, eye contact.

38% of the impression we make on others is determined by what they HEAR, that is, the tone and pitch of the voice, the pace and use of pause, clarity of speech, accent.

7% of the impression we make on others is determined by the WORDS they hear.

Research among television viewers backs up these statistics. We are far more influenced by how someone looks and sounds than by what they say. We use appearance and non-verbal behaviour to judge others more immediately than actions and words, and when we are not clear what actions and words mean we use what we see and hear for clarification.

Let's take an example:

A man bumps into you in the street. He stops and says 'Sorry' (actions and words). He does not look at you as he speaks and he shakes his head in an aggressive manner. His body is angled away from you and his chest is puffed up. His fists are clenched, his chin is thrust forward and his face is registering annoyance. His voice sounds tense, and he delivers 'sorry' quickly and sharply as a reprimand.

Another man bumps into you in the street. He stops and says 'Sorry'. He looks at you when he speaks and cranes his face towards you. He angles his body towards you and rounds his shoulders, lowering his height a little. He raises his hands and makes a gesture of appeasement, showing you the palms of his hands. He looks concerned and his voice sounds conciliatory. He delivers 'sorry' softly and slowly.

How we make a first impression matters more than what we say.

SELF-CONSCIOUSNESS

A ctually, it was not until I was 40 that I was able to go into a room and say to myself: 'What do I think of these people?' Before that, I had always thought: 'What do these people think of me?' When I became 40, I said to myself, 'You are either a whole person now, or you never will be. Believe in yourself.' – Brooke Astor

Has anyone *never* felt self-conscious?

Self-consciousness can strike at unexpected moments, and can be an uncomfortable reminder of a past experience, when the critical 'inner voice' goes into action.

People who are very self-conscious are painfully aware of their shortcomings. They may imagine these shortcomings to be considerably worse than they are. This heightened sense of inadequacy may cause them to blush, to appear defensive, to remember their physical and intellectual limitations. They may find it impossible to sit still in a chair, or may stumble over their words. The critical voice inside their head is likely to be working overtime. When self-consciousness manifests itself in this way, the projected image, that of an embarrassed, uncomfortable person, is a fairly accurate reflection of what is happening on the inside.

Some people compensate for feeling self-conscious on the inside by projecting a very different image to the outside. Someone who is constantly titivating with her appearance for instance, who is constantly drawing attention to her hair and body, may come across to others as 'vain and self-obsessed', yet her behaviour is an expression of a sense of inadequacy in her self-image. Another person may be shy on the inside, yet the signals he sends to others via lack of eye contact, apparent lack of interest, will mean that others judge him as 'arrogant and inconsiderate'.

The self-conscious person is highly aware of scrutiny, acutely aware that he or she is being 'judged' by others. In some situations, like public speaking, presentations or interviews, this sense of 'being under scrutiny' is considerably heightened. Usually there is more than one person doing the scrutinising and the decisions taken during and after the event may be significant, with far-reaching effects.

Young children are not self-conscious; it is something we learn to be as we get older. It is worth examining your past to try and understand where you got the feeling from. Perhaps your parents rarely gave you praise and approval and you expect others either to fail to notice your achievements or to reject you. Maybe you were a fat child, and were teased about it a great deal, and since then have been embarrassed when others look at your body. Or you may have been brought up in a family where there was a lot of pressure to conform, to fit in and be acceptable; maybe you are not comfortable expressing your individuality and making yourself prominent. Several influences are likely to affect your attitude.

Practically, what can you do about self-consciousness? You need to consider that when you are feeling self-conscious, you are displaying *an unrealistically generous attitude towards others*. You are assuming (wrongly, on most occasions, I think) that *other people are very interested in you*.

You are assuming that *you are being given far more attention than is likely*. Let's take a situation in which many people feel self-conscious, standing on a platform just before making a speech. You are under scrutiny and you have little to do, which makes the situation worse. What are the audience thinking? Are they giving you all their attention and analysing the signals you are sending out? Are they very interested in you, and what you have to say? Do you have their focused concentration? Or are they also pondering such issues as: Did I double-lock the front door? Shall I have chops or steak this evening? Are they going to put the air conditioning on in here? Point made, I hope.

It is commonly assumed that extroverts find speaking in public and meeting new people easier than introverts. Extroverts, as described in Chapter Two, focus outwards on their external reality. Psychologists have had some success in helping people who feel chronically self-conscious by getting them to run an 'inner monologue' which focuses outwards on others. So, when you go into a situation where you feel self-conscious, stimulate your interest in others present. Ask yourself about them; for instance, how may people are wearing spectacles? do the men have beards? are the women wearing lipstick? Concentrate on *other people's presentation*: how old are they? what values do their appearances exemplify? what mood are they in? If necessary, if you are acutely self-conscious, learn the last three questions and keep running them through your head and supplying the answers. This focus on the 'others' also helps you tune in to what you are saying and how you are going to say it, so that you make your message more appropriate to the needs of your 'judges'.

Another way of approaching self-consciousness, is to think less of the *effect* you are making and more about *what you are doing*. Some of us have a strong fatalistic streak, and we habitually expect dire outcomes. We live in the gloomy future, not the present. Fear of what may happen determines our lives. Others among us blow the past up out of all proportion. We allow an influence or experience to dominate our present responses far too much. Keep asking yourself what am I *doing* now? rather than concerning yourself with the *effect* you are making. Stop thinking that this situation is inevitably going to go wrong, or this situation is inevitably going to repeat a bad past experience. Stay with your *action in the present*. If your means of presentation are appropriate, your ends will look after themselves. Think of how you are coming over in terms of active verbs, actions that you perform to others. So when you enter a room full of strangers for instance, you could be smiling and acknowledging others and welcoming them into your company. You may be reassuring them that it is all right to approach you and talk. You can perform all these actions, before you speak a word.

Ask yourself, in what situations do you become self-conscious? Some people, for instance, hate the phone, and may well benefit from some voice training so that they learn to like the way they sound. Others do not like standing in front of groups because of poor body image, or because they do not know how to choose clothes that suit them. These problems can be tackled.

Learning to control the outward symptoms of self-consciousness can be a great help. At least others are not seeing that you feel uncomfortable. Sections in Chapter Four on body language and Chapter Six on voice should help you. For women a green-based moisturiser may counteract blushing, and either sex can dress to conceal flushing of the neck.

Remember that your physical symptoms feel far worse to you than they look to others. At least you are showing sensitivity, even if it is heightened. Most of us prefer a sensitive person to someone who fails to notice the delicacy of other people and situations.

MEETING NEW PEOPLE

Highly accomplished, intelligent, well-balanced people can find meeting others difficult. Consider the following:

- Your non-verbal signs indicate that you are accessible to others. And other people will show you that you may get involved with them. A group of people at a party are talking, but in a desultory way; they are standing with plenty of space between them and a couple of them keep letting their eye contact wander around the room; then you may judge that you can ask 'May I join you?' Smiling and making eye contact with others indicates that you would like to meet them.

- Activity, like shaking hands and making contact through touch, going to get someone a drink or hanging up their coat, gives us 'something to do' and can cover up the embarrassment of each person assessing the other. You take the initiative and role of leader, indicating confidence when you offer your hand to someone else.

- Many of us are brought up with the advice 'never talk to strangers'. When we become adults, learning to talk to strangers is a necessary skill. Small talk indicates that you are prepared to get involved with another person. It is a means of gently establishing that you have common ground with the other person.

- If you are panicking, look around the room and ask yourself: 'Who looks most like me?' Not necessarily in physical terms, but in attitude, clothing signals, body language. Remember the 'people like us' factor.

- The key to feeling comfortable meeting others is to *show interest in them*. We can do this through asking questions, or by making statements about a topic that is generally relevant to everyone. Depending on your personality, you will feel more comfortable with one style than the other.

- If we question someone, it should not sound like an interrogation. Questions should not be of too personal or probing a nature, or you may appear intrusive. When the other person is finding it difficult to talk, a statement revealing something about yourself can make them feel that they can be more forthcoming – 'I was worried I wouldn't be here on time' or 'I don't know many people here', for instance. Too much disclosure, however, may frighten the other person off.

- We British always talk about the weather because it is something that everyone experiences. Comments about the event itself, or the surroundings or the people or occasion that have prompted the event are good openers.

- Traditionally, when introducing people to one another, the lower status or younger person was introduced to the higher status or older person. It is very helpful to introduce people giving some information that can stimulate conversation: 'This is Sarah, who's just qualified as an accountant', 'This is John, he's Mary's cousin and he lives in the States', for example.

- Conversation depends on turn-taking and generosity. As well as letting the other person have their say, it is important to be responsive to all the non-verbal signals they are using which tell you a great deal about them.

MEN AND WOMEN

In the last thirty years, there have been considerable changes in the way men and women regard each other's roles. And the 'total image' of each sex has changed too. In the sixties, following the 'liberation' of the pill, the advent of unisex fashion meant that men and women started to present themselves in very similar ways. Men adopted 'feminine' styles of long hair, floral patterns and paisley; for women boyish clothes and gamine haircuts became fashionable. In the seventies, punks were often indistinguishable from one another in terms of gender, while women started to 'power dress', wearing clothes that sometimes made them look like imitation men. Our eighties men and women have been conformist and conservative, with the rise to prominence of women in the workplace showing effect; we've seen a softer 'new man', and a woman who, while dressing in tailored clothes, often has long flowing locks. The 1990s, with predicted growth in female employment and increasing concern with green issues, seem likely to further the blurring of traditional sex roles.

Social conditioning still affects the 'total image' a man or woman presents to the world, and the way we respond to one another on first impressions. Many of us still associate power with masculinity and find it difficult to reconcile power and femininity. It is therefore easier to be a physically large man in our society than it is to be a small man, size being equated with power and significance. By the same token, it is easier to be a small woman than a large one. Small people, after all, appear vulnerable and make others want to protect them.

Conditioning also makes it easier for a man to demonstrate introvert qualities and a woman to be more extrovert. We like men to be 'strong, silent types' and they are conditioned to have decided views and opinions, to have clear goals, and to be less concerned with what others think of them and more concerned with achievement. A man often defines himself almost exclusively by what he does.

Women, on the other hand, are brought up to concern themselves far more with relationships. They are expected to make themselves look physically attractive, and to be responsive to the needs of others. The roles of mother, wife and daughter require them to develop their caring and nurturing capacities, and they often define them as much in terms of family relationships as by what they do. Many women want to balance their need for personal achievement with their biological needs and the fulfilment that comes from motherhood.

'Little boys don't cry.' In many families, only little girls are allowed to show emotion. If you show emotion, you reveal vulnerability, and for men this is socially unacceptable. Men indicate power, and therefore masculinity, by being more distant and less expressive. They often use less facial expression than women, and tend to express what they are thinking rather than feeling. With 'inner reality' dominant, they will not 'tune in' to others to the extent that women will. Men will often talk more, listen less effectively and be more inscrutable than women. They may put a higher value on what words indicate than on non-verbal signals. Men are more likely to regard their appearance as of minor importance. On first impressions a man may be most concerned with establishing his power and self-possession.

Women are generally thought to do well in jobs requiring 'people skills'. Years of conditioning in focusing out on others may mean that they have greater awareness of non-verbal signals than men. Because women are encouraged to be expressive and responsive they often reveal far more readily what they are thinking and feeling. In situations like negotiation this can be detrimental. Sometimes, in their desire to identify and win approval, women can appear submissive, talking less, listening with great attention and being very generous to others. They may be very concerned with the 'right' appearance, and they have greater scope for getting this wrong (because of the wide variety of women's clothing available). On first impressions, a women may often be most concerned with reacting to others and gaining their approval.

Both sexes can learn to adapt their 'total image' so that they become more flexible in dealing with one another. Men can improve their understanding of others and develop interpersonal skills; women can learn to improve the way they convey self-possession and power. We can learn from each other.

To make the most of that vital first impression, you need to be able to control the signals that you relay to others. These signals need to be consistent; otherwise your total image will not work. If your appearance is immaculate but your speech slipshod, others will get a confused message. It is possible to appear both confident and accessible; savouring your individuality, but also receptive to involvement with others. The following chapters show you how.

chapter four

BODY TALK

Y our body talks, and the way you use your body and face determines the success of your total image. You may be expensively dressed from head to toe, but if you are unable to keep still and your eye contact is shifting relentlessly, then you will look ill-at-ease. You may be super-fit and in great shape, but if your posture is habitually defensive, then other people will not feel at ease in your company. Remember, behaviour breeds behaviour.

Body language can even affect the image you convey through your voice, especially over the telephone. If you tend to slump you will inhibit the efficiency of your breathing and your voice will not sound as powerful and controlled as it could do.

The good news is that much of our body language is governed by habits, which can be changed. Very often we are not aware of the signals we have become accustomed to sending out. We have been using the habits for years and they have become second nature. Through identifying them, and consciously adopting alternative behaviour in their place, we can stop them spoiling our self-presentation.

Our bodies respond to our minds. Under stress, our mouths dry up, our shoulders hunch, our stomachs churn, our knees tremble. Physical reactions confirm and exaggerate our thoughts and feelings. And if we are under extreme stress, or stress over a long period of time, we suffer physical collapse. The mind also has the power to heal the body, as demonstrated by instances of people recovering from apparently incurable diseases. It can also will the body to perform incredible feats of great physical strength and endurance.

Our attitudes and emotional responses are governed by habit and we show them through our physical appearance. In *Families and How to Survive Them* by Robin Skynner and John Cleese, the latter comments:

These habitual emotions will show themselves in posture, facial expressions and the typical way they [people] move. Take a depressive person. He'll tend to slump and slouch and move apathetically. And by virtue of having his face in a depressed expression over the years, he'll develop certain facial lines which we recognise immediately. The same applies to a cheerful fellow who smiles a lot – he'll get laugh lines, and will usually move in a more positive, eager, upright kind of way; somebody a bit manic will move jerkily and seem tense and tend to have staring eyes.

Spoken language seems to indicate how we understand this mind–body connection. You can 'twist someone's arm', 'shoulder a lot of responsibility', 'break your lover's heart'. One branch of therapy called Bioenergetics, developed by Alexander Lowen and based on the work of the controversial therapist Wilhelm Reich, goes so far as to say that certain emotions are 'stored' in different parts of the body, creating a protective armour. The jaw may store unhappiness; the chest, neglect; the shoulders, too much responsibility. We express these stored emotions by tension and immobility in the corresponding parts of the body.

Sometimes a physical habit can be a reflection of 'you in the past' rather than 'you in the present'. You may have had a period of several years when for most of the time you had a defeatist attitude towards life. Perhaps your mental attitude has changed. But unless you have consciously done something about it, your body language and bearing may still carry that care-ridden attitude.

The whole package of facial, bodily and vocal demeanour is (often) termed a person's 'physical use'. We learn much of physical use from our parents. A child will often walk like a parent and have similar posture and body language. Levels of 'expressiveness' are learned, too: the extent to which you use your body and face to express things and the extent to which you limit demonstration. And the culture into which you were born will affect this. If you were born and raised in Italy you are likely to be much more expressive than if you come from the English Home Counties.

Even between people from similar cultural backgrounds who speak the same language, if there is wide variance between their levels of expression, misunderstandings may arise:

Derek had been asked to prepare a report detailing changes necessary to make his department more efficient. When his new boss, Nadia, costed the changes she realised that she would have to tell Derek that his scheme was impractical. Derek is very expressive, a 'people' person and very responsive to others. Nadia is very self-contained, uses little gesture and even less facial expression. When Nadia describes her objections and counter-proposals, Derek leans forward in his chair, nods his head a lot and smiles. It is his intention to indicate through his behaviour that he is encouraging Nadia to keep talking – he always does that when he listens to other people. Nadia assumes that Derek is indicating that he agrees with the *content* of what she is saying. At the end of her case she says: 'So you agree with everything I've said, then?' Derek is dumbfounded.

Expressiveness has a lot to do both with the need to get involved with others and the need to assert your individuality – your 'separateness'.

The amount of expression you use in your body language can indicate the extent to which you wish to get reaction from others, or the extent to which you wish to distance yourself. Extremes of either, as demonstrated in the above example, create barriers in communication.

You use your face and body in a way that is highly distinctive and individual. When we watch impersonators on television, we usually find it easy to identify their subjects even before we hear anything. The impersonator will have taken a physical habit and caricatured it.

You create an impression on others through the size and shape of your body. You can gain or lose muscle or fat, and is also possible, of course, to alter your 'apparent' size through the use of body language and clothing, but your skeletal framework is fixed. Human beings come in three different basic shapes, dictated by heredity: ectomorphs are slight and straight-figured, mesomorphs have broader shoulders and compact, muscular frames, and endomorphs are pear-shaped with shorter, broader bottom halves. Muscle and fat on these frames will build up your shape and frame.

Instinctively and stereotypically we judge others by their size. Thin people are assumed to be intelligent, intense, possibly neurotic; those with muscular, athletic bodies are regarded as dynamic and aggressive; and plump people are often thought of as good-humoured and relaxed. These interpretations are irrational, but many of us persist in using them.

TENSION

When we 'read' one another, body language is a most potent source of revelation. We respond strongly to it, not always consciously. If someone's words and voice are not conveying credibility, then it is their body language that will make us decide whether to trust them or not. Your physical use is a powerful indication to others of how tense or relaxed you are. Some people have a high level of physical tension most of the time; with most of us it varies according to whether we feel under stress or not. Someone with a tense body finds it difficult to keep still, arms and legs twitching even when sitting or standing in a fairly relaxed situation. It is very difficult to feel relaxed in the company of someone who has this level of tension. Occasionally, in my work, I've met tense individuals who have described themselves as 'extremely energetic'. Tension *is* a form of energy, but it is energy that is misplaced and misdirected. When you are tense, you are wasting energy to little constructive purpose.

Learning physical relaxation will help you get in tune with the responses of your body, and sense when you are starting to tense. You can get familiar with the sensations of relaxed muscles as opposed to tense ones. When you start to seize up with tension, you can instruct those muscles to recall the sensation of relaxation. To do this effectively, relaxation exercises need to be done on a regular basis.

General Relaxation Exercises

Do these exercises if:

- you are often physically tense, and find it difficult to sit or stand still for any length of time.

- you have an important presentation or interview to do later in the day, and you feel very nervous.

1. Sitting down, go through the body part by part, starting with the toes. Tense your toes and relax them completely. Tense your ankles, then relax them completely. Continue up through the body. Take your time to do this exercise, close your eyes if it helps, and make sure each part is completely relaxed before your moved on to another area.

2. Standing up, stretch your arms to the ceiling. Stand on tiptoe to stretch yourself out as much as you can. Then, working through the body from the fingers and wrists, start relaxing the body from the top, first letting the hands flop, then the arms from the elbow, then the upper arms and so on. Let the body flop so that you hang over dropped from the waist. Check that your knees are bent slightly and that you are breathing easily. Get comfortable flopping over and bounce gently in that position. Sense that you are stretching out your spine then return gently and smoothly to a standing position, gradually working through the spine vertebra by vertebra as you rise. (See opposite.)

Stretch to the ceiling.   Relax your body.

Flop, with knees bent.

3. Kneeling on the floor, get into a foetal position. Allow your weight to rest on your legs with your head on the floor in front of your body, so that you are in a collapsed 'S' shape. Breathe easily. (This position can help ease backache caused by curving the small of the back inwards in the opposite direction to the position assumed in the exercise.)

The S-shape.

4. Lie on the floor, with a book or a cushion under your head. Sense that you are flattening your back on the floor as much as you can without straining. Bend your legs so that your knees come up and point at the ceiling, but not so much that the small of the back starts to lift off the floor. Flop all your weight on to the floor, try to release any tense muscles that seem to be holding your body in a certain position. Breathe easily, taking time to let the breath drop easily in to the body and then blowing slowly out.

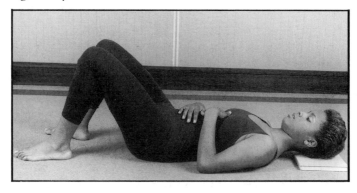

A relaxed pose.

5. Try 'creative visualisation'. Lie down in a warm, darkened room with your eyes closed. Imagine you are somewhere very pleasant, on a warm beach, or in a bath of warm oil. Savour all the sensory pleasures that this situation has to offer, what you can see, sense and smell. If you have problems conjuring up images, then you could want to record a description of the situation and play it while you relax.

6. Buy some ready-made relaxation tapes and listen to them on a regular basis.

7. If you are feeling too agitated to relax, make a list of all the things you have to do, and prioritise them.

8. Book yourself regular massage or learn to do it yourself, from a book or preferably classes.

POSTURE

We tend to associate the word 'posture' with old-fashioned deportment classes. Your posture is really the attitude you present to the world: how you regard yourself, how life has treated you and how you feel in the current situation. Good posture is not about exaggeratedly upright bearing as taught by the army; it is about the natural alignment of the head and spine, with the body free of tension and 'locking'.

Your posture will be governed by habits that have become permanent. If you thrust your chin forward every time you speak, fairly typical of an aggressive, go-ahead personality, then you will start to feel comfortable and normal in that position (see page 50). Your spine will start to look permanently curved at the neck. In the same way, if you always round your shoulders or puff out your chest, then these positions will start to feel familiar and natural.

Were you to realign your posture, it would feel odd. Your reflection in a mirror would look strange, because your accepted notion of yourself is of someone who has a particular quirk. This is why we find it difficult to be objective about the posture we use.

We learn postural 'quirks' from our parents, but our posture is also affected by our emotional state and how we adapt to physical conditions. If you sit at a badly designed desk and chair for most of the day, and you have to curve your spine to get comfortable, then this will have an effect.

Often we develop little habits because of our bodies and appearance. Someone who is deaf in one ear, for instance, will listen extra-hard with

Thrusting the head forward.

A natural alignment.

the other ear, which can lead them to tilt their head to one side. If for several years you had long hair that fell over one eye, then you could have developed the habit of flicking the hair back from the face and again tilting the head to one side. If you are tall, and felt self-conscious about the fact when you were younger (many habits are formed in the sensitive teen years), you could have developed the habit of stooping, in an attempt to make yourself look smaller and get down to the level of we lesser mortals.

Your bearing is very much affected by the desire to make yourself or bits of yourself look smaller or bigger. You can indicate through your posture how much 'right' you feel you have to be somewhere, and how significant you consider your presence. We see this indication demonstrated most effectively by the positions most of us will adopt when we are on our best behaviour. We will sit symmetrically, with our legs together, body upright, hands folded in lap maybe. If someone took a photograph or drew a picture of us, and encircled our body shape with a pencil, we would not be taking up a significant amount of space. In a relaxed position, with legs crossed to the side, maybe, body leaning back and slanting, an arm stretched out along the back of the chair, which is taking lots of weight, we appear far more expansive. Were the body shape in this photo to be circled with a pencil, the amount of space occupied would be far more significant (see page opposite).

We can try to change the apparent shape of our bodies through the way we use posture. A short, podgy person who habitually slumps will, of course, draw attention to his or her size. Another person of similar build but with good posture will create a quite different effect. You could want to disguise a bulging stomach by habitually holding and tensing it in. This will thrust the top half of the body forward and create the effect that you are top-heavy.

*Left: Looking 'small' and
insignificant.
Below: Relaxed and
confident and taking up a lot
of space.*

Fashion and whims of society can have an effect on posture. High heels, tight-fitting fashions or loose-fitting shapes will all affect the wearers' posture. Certain body shapes become fashionable at different times, the voluptuous siren shape of the fifties, for example, giving way to the stick-like waif of the sixties. Your body feels a certain way in different clothes, and holds itself accordingly. If fashion and society are promoting and preoccupied with a certain ideal, the peace-loving hippy or the Hollywood screen goddess, those who aspire to these ideals could well reflect their aspirations through floppy relaxed bearing or pouting lips and thrusting breasts. Currently it is fashionable to have an athletic, well-exercised shape.

The posture you adopt can also indicate how you have responded to stress. Under pressure, human beings have a 'flight or fight' instinct, that is, we feel an urge either to quit the scene or to take on all comers. Indications of the 'flight' instinct include pulling the head back and up, literally lifting the nose for take-off; tensing the shoulders and holding the arms stiffly by the side (getting the wings ready); and dancing about on the spot (coming out of the hangar). We see the 'fight' instinct in thrusting the head forward, bending elbows and clenching fists ready for battle, letting arms spread to the side and standing with legs wide apart, to make yourself look bigger and therefore more threatening. (See opposite.) Again, if these habits occur frequently enough they become permanent features of our presentation.

Your posture shows then, to an extent, how you protect yourself and sends out signals accordingly. Whether we 'fight or flee' depends of course on the situation. Many of us, though, tend to use one response more than the other. We fail to appreciate that signals formed by the 'fight' response that make someone look aggressive arise from a sense of being threatened:

On a training course we were working with a group on the signals they send out through their posture. We do an exercise which quickly identifies each individual 'flight or fight' response. John, short, compact and extremely muscular, pulled his head right back and thrust his chin forward, making him look aggressive and threatening. I mentioned these signals. At coffee-time he said that he had always been a very shy, nervous person and studied martial arts to help him deal with this. Ever since he could remember, he had felt that quite a lot of other people felt nervous in his presence. For the first time he realised that his physical response to his feelings of inadequacy made him intimidate others. The identification of these misleading signals was a complete revelation to him.

Fight: Our model is standing his ground.

Flight: Our model is wishing he wasn't there.

Your posture shows the ageing process. The more you assimilate bad habits, particularly slumping, then the older you will look. Poor posture can also affect your health: if the spine is misaligned you risk backache, and it cannot be good for the internal organs to be compressed as some of them are for hours at a time. When you slump you will look tired and de-energised. This obvious ageing need not happen as much as it does. Elderly practitioners of the Alexander Technique, the study of the use of the body and alignment of the spine, look upright and energised. They are the best advertisement for the technique which was developed by an actor, F. M. Alexander, because he kept losing his voice. If you wish to improve your posture and the way you use your body, try the Alexander Technique. It is a slow and gentle process, because changing old habits cannot be done overnight.

You can change your posture, and also identify those habits that send out potent signals that are detrimental to your presentation. If you would rather these signals read differently, you can do something about it. Every one of us holds tension in various parts of the body, from the person who has permanently tense shoulders and actually *sleeps* with them tense (remarkably easy to do) to the person whose stomach churns when the time comes to speak in front of a group of people. Tension travels rapidly through the body; if you clench your fist, then feel the muscles in the top of your arm, you will find that they are tense. Continue clenching your fist and you will feel and see that your jaw is tensing too. Tense areas of the body are often hotter than the rest of the body when you touch them.

If you identify your particular tense areas, then you can do something about them. You probably know to some extent where you take your tension – it will be the area that reacts when under stress. So if your knees start wobbling (a common site of tension, particularly for small people who lock their knees in an attempt to look taller), then you know that is an area you need to learn to relax.

When we control our physical symptoms of tension, it is conceivable that our tension level drops because the mind is no longer receiving signals that confirm the state. And also, of course, other people can't see that we are nervous, which is reassuring.

Here are descriptions of the common sites of tension, how they affect the way we communicate and what signals they send out to others. There are also exercises to help alleviate the tension. Often simply thinking about relaxing an area can help, particularly if you have been doing these exercises and are 'in touch' with the difference between the sensation of tense and relaxed muscle.

Posture Exercises

Do these exercises if:

- your general posture needs improving.

- under pressure and scrutiny, you 'shrink' or 'puff up' through physical tension.

- you feel generally physically shaky when you are nervous.

1. Stand on the balls of the feet, letting the arms hang loosely by the sides. Gradually lower the heels, keeping the weight slightly forward (about two-thirds on the balls of the feet). Try to retain the feeling of being tall and well-balanced as you lower the heels, with the sensation of being suspended from a string which is pulling you up at the top of your head.

2. Stand against a wall and feel the back of the head, shoulder blades, bottom, and backs of heels are contacting the wall. Adjust your body so that you feel relaxed and balanced in this position. Walk away from the wall, keeping a sense of length in the spine and head.

3. Deliberately slump, allowing the ribs to sink inwards and the shoulders to grow round. Grow outwards and upwards as you come to a good standing position feeling taller and wider. Shake your arms and legs to relieve tension, check that the elbows, knees and ankles are relaxed.

4. When sitting, always sit well back in the chair and make sure that you have got as much of the small of your back as possible supported by the back of the chair.

Your Head and Neck

When we communicate we usually look at one another's neck and head. The back of the neck is an extremely common site of tension. Someone who is irritating you can literally be a 'pain in the neck'; very often when a person is tired or tense they will raise an arm and rub the back of the neck, an indication of where they are taking the tension even if they are not conscious of it.

If you take tension here you could thrust your chin forward every time you speak as described earlier. (Winston Churchill did this, and Neil Kinnock has a tendency to do it.) The habit makes the neck seem shorter as the head is being pulled in to the body – it looks bullish, in fact. You might tilt your head to one side which will lend you an enquiring air, well removed from an appearance of power and resolution. If you drop your head down towards the chest frequently, then you'll convey an impression of shyness, self-effacement, possibly even fear. These habits are likely to become accentuated when you are speaking with others and feeling 'observed', entering a crowded party, speaking at a meeting, or meeting someone for the first time.

Try to look at yourself objectively in the mirror or get a friend or relative to help you. Your spine does curve at the neck (which is why in the relaxation exercises on the floor earlier in this chapter I suggested putting a book or cushion under the head, to support the natural bend). Establish whether your automatic response is to thrust the head forward or tilt the chin upwards; many of us make these responses every time we speak or use effort.

When your head feels comfortable and natural in a central position, there will be no locking or strain in the neck or throat and your total image will benefit.

Exercises for Neck Tension

1. Gently and smoothly nod the head, like those nodding dogs we used to see in the back windows of cars. Your aim is to stretch out the neck and release the tension. When you have established a smooth, almost hypnotic movement and you sense your neck is relaxed, walk across the room, still nodding your head gently. Many people thrust their heads forward when they walk, leading with the head and creating tension. The exercise should prevent this.

2. Massage the back of the neck, using a circular movement on the two large muscles running from the top of the back to the back of the head. If the muscles feel hard they are tense; they should 'soften up' as you massage them. Many beauty salons now offer neck and back massages for men and women, which can work wonders for these areas. The service is usually reasonably cheap and does not take up a great deal of time.

3. Gently revolve the head, keeping the face forward rather than twisting it to the side, The aim is to stretch and release the neck muscles rather than twisting them. Change direction.

4. Let the head drop on to the chest. Remember, an average head is said to weigh about ten pounds. Link the hands and place them on the back

of the head to help stretch out the neck. Adjust your neck and shoulders, so that you get comfortable in that position and focus on slow breaths as you breathe OUT.

The Shoulders

Some of us seem to 'carry the world' on our shoulders. The neck and shoulders are close together, and if you have tension in one area then it is likely to spread to another. If you tense of the back of your neck, creating an exaggerated curve at the top of the spine, the shoulders will start to round. The shoulders are a relatively large area in the body and tension can quickly carry from them into the arms, hands and fingers, which is why so many of us find it impossible to stand with our hands and arms relaxed at our sides: we drum fingers on our thighs or clench our fists tightly.

The shoulders are a prime site of tension for many people and will look slightly raised and forward all the time. If you are one of these, then telling yourself *shoulders down and back* whenever you can, particularly when you are doing things like sitting on a train, walking along the street, or driving, can help. Try to make the response habitual. The shoulders are important in 'impression management', which is why padded shoulders in clothes lend people an aura of power. The shoulders are the hanger if you like, from which the rest of the body is suspended. Look carefully at speakers on television (particularly those talking about a crisis or who are being cross-examined) and you'll train yourself to spot shoulder tension. Tension in the chest and shoulder blades also will be helped by these exercises.

Exercises for Shoulder and Chest Tension

1. Raise the shoulders and drop them, making sure that you release the tension completely when you let them go. 'Walk' them up to your ears, alternately moving each one degree by degree. Then let them go completely.

2. Roll the shoulders gently backwards, stretching out the chest muscles, and forwards, spreading the shoulder blades. Five times forwards and five times backwards. In between, check by nodding the head that you have not created tension in the neck.

3. Bring the arms up in front of the chest and link the hands. Without raising the shoulders, stretch the arms forward and release the shoulder blades.

4. Link the hands behind the back and stretch arms away and upwards from the body. Try and sense that you are releasing tension from the chest and the shoulder blades.

5. People with a lot of chest tension will often look slightly puffed up – this stance can make them look self-important. A common response to panic is to put a hand on the chest as though trying to appease it. Curving the spine so that the chest collapses and then releasing the curl so that the shoulders release right back and down and the chest muscles release can help.

The Stomach

Unfortunately, you don't get a flat stomach by tensing it. You might give yourself a churning sensation when you get nervous or, even worse, feel sick and have to rush to the loo. You get a flat stomach by exercising regularly, doing things like sit-ups, not by gripping it in with tension. If you do hold a lot of tension in your stomach, then the breathing exercises in Chapter Six will help, as will consciously thinking about releasing the area.

The Legs

If you habitually tense in your knees, locking them, then you will be putting pressure on your back. With tense legs, the small of the back curves too much, and the stomach area is thrust out. You'll look as though the middle part of your body is tipping forward. If you are used to standing with your legs locked, then it feels very strange to stand with the 'brake' knocked off. You minimise the risk of lower back ache by reminding yourself to stand like this whenever you can.

Shake out your legs and arms before you go into a demanding situation. Before interviews, presentations, important meetings, your body needs warming up as much as your mind needs preparation. Others are going to make judgements about you based on your posture and body language.

Lyn and Sally are similar to look at; they are both small, slight with short dark hair. Lyn moves in a slow, languid way, never appearing to rush. Sally, on the other hand, moves in a quick, precise, bird-like manner. Before either of them speaks, people form very different impressions of them; their friends regard Lyn as relaxed, easy-going, even lazy, while they think of Sally as energetic, efficient, often tense.

We can characterise movement by thinking about its speed, its direction and the posture of the mover. If you are ill-at-ease in a situation you are likely to move quickly, jerkily because you would like to get out of the situation. We often move quickly if we think we are being boring. Slow, ponderous movement can indicate indecisiveness and lack of energy.

If you are happy with your body and fairly relaxed, your movement will be energised and flowing. You won't rush or twitch. You'll be happy to take up a lot of space. Many of us have distinctive walks, leading movement with a particular part of the body. At school, there was one girl who was inexplicably popular with the boys. All of us tried to figure out what made her such an attraction, but to little avail. Years later, when I recalled this girl, I remembered that she always moved as though her pelvis was leading her, which gave her a suggestive air and threw her hip area into prominence.

Each of us has a particular style of movement. Some people move in straight lines, in terms of both the direction in which they move the whole body and individual gestures. Others have far curvier, sinuous movement patterns. Some of you will always be moving forward, with head and gestures. Others use more expansive gestures to the side and seem to spread themselves wherever they go. Some people tend to pull themselves upwards when they move, and their gestures will be made high in the body.

When you are talking to someone who objects or changes attitude towards what you are saying, he or she will invariably move. The listener might just adjust posture slightly, maybe shift weight from one buttock to another or perhaps use a definite gesture like stroking the chin. Either way, unless they are very aware of body language, you could detect their reaction to what you are saying. It goes without saying that unnecessary movement wastes energy.

It is worth cultivating the 'art of stillness'. If you can keep relatively still, particularly under pressure, you'll appear composed and have the effect of reassuring others. Just try sitting absolutely still, focus on your breathing, check through your body for any tension areas. Let it relax.

GESTURES

Some gestures, such as pointing, kissing, shaking hands, are done consciously. Others, such as nose-rubbing, foot-tapping, ear-scratching, are unconscious actions. Every day you perform hundreds of gestures that show how you feel and send out signals to others.

It is important when interpreting gestures to put them into context. Posture, positioning and the speed and energy of gestures matter. If you slump back in a chair and shake your fist, the gesture will not have the threatening quality it would have if you sat upright, leaning forward in the chair. Waving your finger at somebody in a slow, relaxed manner could indicate that you were saying 'I told you so'; wagging your finger with speed and energy could be a far more severe reprimand. Human beings are rarely still; we usually move from one gesture to another. We should bear this in mind when interpreting gestures from photographs, drawings or film stills.

There is a danger of over-interpretation of body language. You could see someone touching their nose and decide that they were not being as truthful as they could be. In fact, they could just have an itchy left nostril.

Some people, women more than men, move their heads a great deal when they talk. They seem to be looking for an approving response from others. If you watch female impersonators you will see how they exaggerate head movement to make themselves appear more feminine. When you watch two women talking, you often see their heads doing a sort of dance, one moving in one direction and then the other one following.

People who convey an impression of single-mindedness, inflexibility, and purpose tend to keep their heads still when they talk, moving just their eyes to look at others. If you look at police spokesmen on television, they often demonstrate this sort of behaviour; it makes them seem powerful and intimidating. If you cut out excessive head movement, fluency of speech increases because your energy is focused. Old news films show that acclaimed orators like Martin Luther King and Enoch Powell were extremely economical with head movement.

If you move your head a great deal, as part of a desire to get approval from others and you want to appear especially powerful in a situation, keep your head movement under control.

The more you feel you need to defend yourself, the more you will protect your 'underbelly', that is, the front of your body. Under attack, the soft, fleshy parts of the body, the breasts and genitals, are the most vulnerable and we instinctively go to defend them. With your underbelly exposed you are vulnerable – but if you look at ease like that, then you look more

Powerful and confident.

Insecure and protective.

Powerful and confident.

Open and relaxed. Underbelly on display.

Defensive and aggressive.

powerful. You protect your underbelly by crossing your ankles or legs, dropping your head, linking your hands in front of your body, folding your arms, raising your hands to your face. When a cat feels secure and trusting, it will roll over and show you its underbelly, so that you can give it a rub. Human beings don't go quite that far, but we do express security and confidence by leaving our underbellies undefended.

Although we defend our bodies because we feel under threat, the gestures we use need not always 'read' to others as insecurity. Folding your arms, for instance, can in a certain situation be taken to indicate aggressive resistance, or blocking off of what is being expressed. It's a gesture that is often used by someone who is being particularly judgemental. If you are persuading another person who is facing you with folded arms and crossed ankles, and they shift position, dropping the hands into the lap and placing the feet flat on the floor, you can assume that they are starting to accept your case.

The less defensive your use of body language, the more powerful, receptive and accessible you appear. Political dignitaries and some members of the Royal Family, particularly on formal occasions, stand and walk with hands clasped behind the back. This is a powerful position, and because the hands are linked nervous mannerisms can be avoided. (Of course, unlike you or me, personages of this standing are usually accompanied by bodyguards, who can rush to protect the royal or political underbelly, if necessary.)

Sometimes we use body language to display our underbellies as a deliberate show of confidence. If you enter a room, and see someone stretched out on a chair, almost as though lying down with their arms raised and hands linked behind the head, their position will convey a 'Hey what are you about, what can you do for me' kind of attitude. There are variations of this position – leaning back, with both arms dangling behind the chair, or sitting asymmetrically with one arm dangling and the other in the lap. It is a high-status position, usually used by men, and it has sexual connotations in that the pelvis and what might be described as 'tackle' is on obvious display. If a woman adopted this position, she would send out signals that she was sexually available. A woman can be intimidated by a man in this position, because it suggests that he is in the role of observer and assessor. Once you realise the extent of display involved, of both underbelly and 'tackle', the position is less threatening.

People on courses often say: 'It's wrong to sit with crossed legs, I know, but I feel comfortable that way. Does it matter?' To my mind, the study of body language should not be 'right' or 'wrong' gestures, rather about using knowledge to convey a positive image and tune in more effectively to others. Much of our use of it is, in any case, instinctive:

Y ou are joining two colleagues in a meeting to discuss how you will work as a team to develop a new project. When you enter the room your two colleagues are sitting with their legs crossed and are leaning forward looking poised for action. You sit down, cross your legs and lean forward in your chair. The meeting goes well.

Showing disinterest and detachment.

Showing involvement through body positions.

If you had entered the room and sat back in your chair with your arms folded, the meeting might not have got off to such a good start. We are attracted to individuals who look like us, not just in terms of physical features, but in attitude. One of the easiest ways to look like another person is to put your body in a similar position. The more you 'mirror' someone else, the greater the rapport. Some sales teams make conscious use of this, adopting very similar body language to that used by the customer. Of course, as customer you can always adopt a strangely interesting posture and see what happens...

We use gestures to reassure ourselves and to channel tension. When you fold your arms across your body you can be performing a kind of 'self-cuddle'; you also make yourself feel warmer. In this position we sometimes rub an arm for further reassurance. We also rub other bits of ourselves, legs, chin, back of neck. We are doing it to tell ourselves 'it's all right really'.

We often use what's been called 'displacement activity' to use up physical tension. Foot-tapping, finger-drumming, chewing gum, twisting bits of hair, nail-biting, are not related to the cause of your tension, but they act as effective ways of venting it. Unfortunately, a lot of these habits can be deeply irritating to others, particularly if they are feeling tense themselves. We use sounds as displacement activity too, the nervous giggle being a good example.

When we perform grooming gestures, tossing hair back, smoothing a skirt, hitching up trousers, fiddling with shirt cuffs or pulling down a jumper, brushing imaginary dust off our clothes, we can be reassuring ourselves and using the gestures as displacement activity. I'm thinking particularly of the sort of behaviour we often perform before entering a room containing strangers, all the minor adjustments we make to the way we look. Frequently we are unaware that we are doing them. Obviously, the more confident you are about your presentation, the less you need to reassure yourself, the lower your tension level and the less you will need to worry, even subconsciously, about your appearance.

SPACE

You are already protecting some of your underbelly in a sitting position, which is why many people dislike standing in front of a group and would prefer to sit. However, if you stand you look bigger because you literally take up more space, and if you look comfortable standing, then you will appear more powerful than if you sat down. We are more decisive when we stand, which is why it has been suggested that if meetings in your office are interminable affairs, then you might introduce the idea of holding them with everybody standing.

Body language can make us look bigger or smaller. If I stand with my hands on my hips and my feet positioned wide apart I will make myself look much bigger, by filling up more space, than if I stood with my toes turning inwards and rounded by shoulders to fold my arms in front of me. If you are expansive in your use of gesture and body positioning, you will seem bigger than you are. This happens time and time again with actors. When you meet them offstage it can be surprising to discover they are actually quite small.

The use of space is important. We all have a bubble of personal space that we move around in, and the radius of these bubbles can vary enormously from individual to individual. A powerful individual looks quite comfortable in space, and takes plenty of it, using expansive gestures. Someone who perceives themselves as less significant, will take up less room. People who feel 'significant' and take up lots of room can easily appear threatening when they come close and intrude upon the space of someone who is not nearly so expansive. It's the 'people like us' factor; if you do not understand someone's use of personal space because it is very different from yours, it can seem threatening.

If you are feeling confident you should be able to stand and sit comfortably in plenty of space, allowing yourself to be observed by others. Dancing about on the spot or foot-twitching indicates that you would like to be out of that particular situation. How much gesture you use depends on your culture and personality. Some nationalities are very expressive and expansive. Even within countries and between classes, there can be considerable differences. In the British Isles for instance, English southerners use less expressive body language than northerners, or the Welsh or Irish.

When you are conducting business with other nationalities, then the more you understand their use of body language and space the better. Michael Argyle, in *The Psychology of Interpersonal Behaviour*, describes an experiment with Arab men, who stand far closer to one another than most other nationalities. The Arab men met two groups of males of other nationalities, one of which had been trained in Arab body language. Of course, the Arabs liked the men in this group far better than the others. If you are doing business internationally, then the more observant and adaptable you can be, the better.

Gestures are most revealing when they contradict what your face and voice are saying. If you are being dishonest you are likely to restrict your use of body language, because it can give you away. When people enjoy talking, and have enthusiasm for their subject, they often use a lot of uninhibited body language.

Some gestures are overtly negative. If someone repeatedly wags a finger at you when they speak, then you will tend to want to react like a naughty schoolchild. Many politicians appreciate this. Here is a list of positive and negative signals that we send out through body language, gesture and positioning. There have been many studies of body language and some of them have put very specific interpretations on gesture. Some of these interpretations are on the wild side, but entertaining, so I've included them in the following list as 'suggested interpretations', which does not mean that I agree with them.

Positive Signals

- Steepling, linking your hands together as though to form a steeple, prevents you making nervous mannerisms. If you have a table in front of you and you have your arms on the table in front of you, with your hands linked, you almost 'stake out territory' for yourself. (Suggested interpretation: confidence and self-possession.)

- Leaving your underbelly unprotected you seem confident and accessible.

- Stillness suggests ease and comfort in a situation, especially the ability to keep hands and feet still and relaxed.

- Gestures showing open palms of hands. (Suggested interpretation: nothing concealed.)

- Sitting asymmetrically demonstrates confidence in taking space.

- Leaning forward indicates interest, but it can also indicate that you are putting in quite a lot of effort and seeking involvement at the expense of your self-possession, and it can therefore lower your status.

- Standing comfortably with your hands and arms relaxed at your side.

- We angle our bodies, and often cross our legs, in the direction of the person that we most like or want to establish rapport with.

- The more empathetic you are with someone, the more likely you are to mirror that person's body language instinctively.

Negative Signals

- Nervous mannerisms: nail-biting, finger- and foot-tapping, playing with hair, gripping or adjusting clothing, patting hair, smoothing eyebrows, chewing gum, smoking.

- Playing with objects and personal effects, pencils, bags, notes, wedding rings. (Suggested interpretation: needing to do something to channel tension.)

- Affectations, like standing and walking with the hand flicked out to the side, suggesting self-consciousness.

- Drawing attention to your sexuality by emphasising certain parts of the body. Women often unwittingly draw attention to their femaleness by standing with the weight on one leg, so that the hips are thrown to the side, drawing an observer's eye to that area.

- Pointing at people, repeating negative gestures, waving your fist or thumping the table with it, showing aggression and tension.

- Touching the face is associated with negative emotions – guilt, self-doubt, irritation. In particular:

Touching the chin and mouth: doubt, reluctance to speak or to accept what is being said. (And it can provoke spots.) People rub their jaws in the way that we rub the back of our necks, as a gesture of needing to relax, the jaw being a very common site of tension.

Touching the nose: said to be an indication of lying.

Touching the eyes: not liking what you are seeing or not wanting to see it any further (suggested interpretation). Putting your hands over your face and eyes is quite a dramatic shutting out, of fear, grief, tiredness.

Touching the ears: not liking what you are hearing (suggested interpretation).

TOUCH

Sometimes, when we are using body language and gestures, touch is involved. How you feel about touching and being touched is as individual as how you feel about personal space. Usually it is the higher status and more powerful person that touches first, as adults feel free to touch children. Sometimes touching can lead to misinterpretation. Someone who touches another person may be actively seeking involvement with that person, who however considers the touch intrusive.

Jane has gone to work for a new company. On her first day at work, her boss Tony comes to enquire how she is getting on. When she says that she is fine, her face looks anxious. Tony, a tactile person, rubs the small of her back, as a reassuring gesture. Jane reacts in two ways; she thinks that Tony is overtly asserting his control over her, reminding her that he is her boss, and she worries whether he might have given her the job because he fancies her.

Don't get the impression that to touch someone is bad, only that it should be used where appropriate and with sensitivity. You could get it wrong if you assume that everyone is as tactile or as undemonstrative as you are. Most of us like being touched. Estee Lauder was of the opinion that if a cosmetics saleswoman touched a customer to stroke on foundation or a sample of perfume, then the customer would buy. Indeed, in some stores you can find your wrists pinioned by over-zealous sales staff as they attempt to spray you with the latest fragrance. It's an appropriate selling technique for that particular business, as women on the whole touch each other far more than men do.

Social and cultural influences play a strong part and the more expressive a race, the more they tend to use touch. Northern Europeans are fairly inhibited in their use of touch. Living in crowded conditions in cities, where there is a high premium on privacy and personal security and where you have to endure the crush of a rush hour, is hardly conducive to readily wanting to make physical contact with each other.

Body Language Exercises

Thanks to technology, one of the best ways of getting feedback about your body language is through observing yourself being interviewed on video. Failing that, these exercises are best done with another person or a mirror.

1. Ask a question moving your head around quite a bit, and then try it keeping your head fairly still. Make the movements as natural as possible and when you keep it still in contrast, check that there is not a slight thrust of the head forward, slight wobble or tilt to the side. Which of these styles comes more easily to you? Most people display one tendency more than the other. See what effects the style with which you are less familiar has on your voice and facial expression.

2. Adopt a sitting position using negative body language that would exclude others and discourage them, and then adopt a position that would include and encourage them. Do the same exercise in a standing position. What are you doing specifically and which of these positions do you habitually assume?

3. Get yourself into positions, sitting and standing, that look open, relaxed and confident, and in which you feel comfortable. Check that your head, neck and shoulders are relaxed and that your back feels wide and long. Memorise these positions. They will be extremely useful in building your total image. When you are under scrutiny, you can adopt these positions with complete confidence.

4. Ask a friend or colleague if you have any irritating mannerisms. If you can persuade them to make an automatic response, like saying 'oops' or something equally irritating every time you use the mannerism, it can produce dramatic improvements. Otherwise, pinning notes instructing you not to perform the mannerism, 'don't twiddle hair' for instance, on your desk, by your phone, near your computer screen can help.

5. Consciously mirror people to try and understand how they are feeling and to use body language to establish greater rapport. Watch others and learn from them. Being naturally curious about other people is the easiest way to become an expert in this subject.

YOUR FACIAL EXPRESSION

Do we get the faces we deserve? If I habitually assume an expression, often enough, will it become etched in the lines of my face? And if so, hadn't I better make sure that this expression is a smile rather than a sneer? The most fine-featured, beautiful faces seem unattractive in a petulant pout or an aggressive scowl. Notice how frown lines, two vertical lines between the eyebrows, make some people appear anxious. The way you hold your head also affects how your face is viewed. If you tilt your head back you are constantly presenting others with what seems to be a snooty expression, if you turn your head to the side slightly, your face could seem to express doubt.

We view faces with considerable prejudice. In court cases, the better-looking defendants are more likely to be found not guilty. We judge people according to their facial characteristics until we get to know them better: thick lips are judged as sensual, thin lips as mean, a high forehead indicates intelligence, small eyes suggest dishonesty. Yet your expression is probably a better guide to your personality than your features.

The extent to which you use facial expression depends on your personality, culture and gender. If you do not readily express emotion, then your face is not going to be very mobile. Some Eastern nationalities show very little emotion and use little facial expression most of the time, though unlike us they will express extreme grief quite openly. In our culture, women are generally more emotionally expressive.

You have to restrict your facial expression to an extent in order to survive. If you wake up one morning feeling enthusiastic and receptive to all the exciting experiences that life has to offer, and saunter down the main road of your town with your face registering this *joie de vivre*, you could end up having experiences very different from the ones you intended. In some jobs, like the police force or the armed forces, showing emotion in extreme situations would be to the detriment of the job. Not surprising, officers in these services develop a 'stiff upper lip' literally. They mask a lot of instinctive expression, and their faces become relatively immobile. We all mask our faces to an extent, though, and if the 'mask' you commonly assume is one of anxiety or irritation, others will judge you accordingly. In Chapter Six we shall see how these 'masks' can affect speech.

Some people find it difficult to smile because they don't like their teeth. Yet a smile is a great asset; remember that behaviour breeds behaviour and when you smile at someone, they feel momentarily happier. We often express tension through our faces, the muscles seizing up and masking natural responses. If you need to convey a quality that you feel you lack naturally, authority for instance, you could impose the appropriate facial expression. This expression can easily become a habit, the manifestation of how insecure you feel about authority. You'll use the expression as a nervous mannerism and it will exclude other expressions. It will limit your apparent receptivity to others. When talking to a subordinate with this bossy expression on your face, you are likely to reduce their confidence. In the same way, people often look judgemental, aggressive or sardonic without realising it.

Sometimes, in an attempt to assert his or her 'separateness' and individuality, a man or woman will become highly inscrutable. In doing this they will appear distant to others, and this may make them feel powerful. There can be a sense of threat about people who reveal very little about themselves. An individual who habitually adopts this mode of presentation will fail to gain trust and confidence. He or she may end up with an enormous amount of pent-up feelings and reactions. In effective, balanced relationships, each person reveals a certain amount about themselves and keeps certain revelations hidden from the other party. We need to build understanding and preserve privacy. However in certain situations, like negotiation for instance, both parties may adopt impassive expressions because they do not want to reveal to the other side what they are really thinking.

If you take a lot of tension in your facial muscles, when you get very nervous or tired your muscles could twitch. In Chapter Six there are exercises to deal with this. When we look at a face, we spend roughly equal amounts of time looking at the mouth and the eyes. Deaf people often make a lot of decisions about people from the way their facial muscles are set, and I've been told by deaf friends that the decisions are usually confirmed. Even a smile can become a nervous mannerism, and send out confusing signals:

Sarah was a manager in local government; she showed great potential, but seemed to be having difficulty standing up for herself. Her boss had sent her on an assertiveness training course, which she enjoyed, and her *content* was more powerful, but her manner was still lacking. She was interrupted, shouted down, and her points were not taken seriously.

Sarah's nervous mannerism was her smile, not an entirely natural smile and she did it all the time. So when she was telling somebody that they could not do something, she smiled. People were very confused by her signals. When her face really relaxed, she was able to use facial expression to reinforce her message.

Nervous mannerisms of the face can be controlled by asking others to let you know when they are happening, by tensing and relaxing the face and massaging the muscles. Here are some common facial mannerisms:

- tensing the forehead, so that you overwork the eyebrows when you communicate. If you raise your eyebrows frequently it is distracting and can lend you a questioning, quizzical air.

- tensing the forehead and frowning.

- thrusting the jaw forward when you communicate, giving an aggressive impression.

- pursing the lips (reading disapproval), pulling them downwards at the sides (reading misery, pouting).

- blinking, screwing up the eyes which can be caused by sight defects or irritation from contact lenses. Blinking can be a pure nervous mannerism, a way of 'shutting things out'.

- blushing – we react to one another according to the colour of the skin on the face. Skin goes white with fear and red with anger. The blusher usually feels worse than an observer: a lot of us feel empathy towards somebody who blushes as it is an indication of their sensitivity.

You can desensitise yourself. Work out the situations or subjects that make you blush, and then prepare yourself. Have four questions about others present, that you are going to ask yourself: 'What body language are they using? What are their faces reading? Do they look comfortable? Can I do anything to make them feel better?' If you focus sufficiently strongly on them, then you are less likely to blush. Don't get disheartened if this doesn't work the first time, as the blushing reaction is well established and you may need several attempts to keep the response under control.

Sometimes a person who blushes can seem threatening to others. As the skin reddens, and a red face is associated with anger, other people may treat you with kid gloves, sensing a potential for explosion. To some eyes it does not register as the embarrassment you feel it to be.

EYE CONTACT

The 'mirrors of your soul' play a most important part in the impression you make. Steady, direct eye contact is essential if you want to put over a confident, honest, receptive image. Generally, men make a lot of steady eye contact when they speak, less when they listen. Women, on the other hand, make good eye contact when they listen but maintain it less when they speak. In some cultures, again in the East, women are conditioned to make little direct eye contact.

If somebody is making little eye contact with you, then you can make one of several assumptions. Firstly, maybe they just don't like you, and that is why they are not acknowledging your presence. In a group of people, the most popular and respected will be looked at more than any other. Secondly, they may simply be shy, and the avoidance of eye contact a nervous mannerism. Thirdly, it's possible they consider themselves above you in status and are therefore not deigning to acknowledge your existence. The fourth reason, and one to look out for: the other person finds you incredibly attractive and doesn't want to risk you spotting their wildly dilating pupils, giving the game away. Finally, most consummate liars understate the need to maintain steady eye contact, but a more naïve liar could avoid it.

When we can't see a person's eyes we are at a disadvantage, because we cannot use eye contact to interpret them. Film and pop stars wear dark glasses, ostensibly to avoid being recognised – but because we can't see their eyes it enhances their mystique and elevates their status.

The right amount of eye contact is important, too. When you are on a bus or a train and the person sitting opposite you stares relentlessly, then you will start to feel very uncomfortable. It is almost as if they are trying to overwhelm you through a deliberate display of power. If your eyes shift very quickly from one person to another, it can raise the tension level of the people, deprive you of clocking their reactions adequately and give the impression that you are not at ease and want the situation to be over.

In recent years, there has been a lot of interest in 'right brain, left brain' thinking. The left side of the brain is said to control structured, logical thinking, while the right side controls emotional and intuitive responses. It has been suggested that if a person's eyes move to the right when they are thinking, then they are using the left side of the brain; if the eyes move to the left, they are using the right side. Other studies have suggested that eye movement can indicate whether a person is thinking with a visual response (in terms of pictures, being very influenced by what they see), an auditory response (in terms of responding strongly to what they hear), or kinaesthetic response (being especially responsive to what they feel, and the sense of touch). Eyes moving upwards to the right or the left or to the centre into middle distance indicate visual orientation, eyes moving to the side, right or left and down to the left indicate an auditory response, and if the eyes are dropping downwards to the right then this suggests a kinaesthetic response. (These movements are described in terms of left and right according to the person making the eyes movements. The sides reverse for left-handers.)

You can easily get into a habit of avoiding eye contact because of shyness. Once you've entered a room without looking at people it is very difficult to start making eye contact. Here are some exercises to make you more aware of the power of eye contact and to help you with difficulties:

Eye Contact Exercises

1. With a friend, take it in turns to ask each other to do something, using steadily maintained eye contact, and then deliberately breaking eye contact mid-request. What different effects does this produce?

2. When you look at people, your eyes should rest on them long enough to acknowledge them as individuals. Silently saying their names to yourself can help get this right.

3. (This exercise, and the one below, are not always comfortable for contact lens wearers.) To help with blinking and twitching muscles around the eyes you need to relax them. Screwing them up and releasing them completely works, as does the following exercise which is very calming.

4. Keeping your head still, gently and slowly, degree by degree, move your eyes in a straight line to the right, then bring them back slowly to the centre. Then in the same way, take them to the left. Bring them back to the centre and fix the eyes comfortably on a point straight ahead. Then move the head, gently and smoothly, degree by degree, to the left, back to the centre and to the right and back to the centre, keeping the eyes straight ahead. Blink to relax the eyes.

chapter five

YOUR APPEARANCE

Grooming and clothes are the packaging of your total image. And in the way that manufacturers pay great attention to the packaging of products in order to get us to buy them, we need to attend to our 'packaging' if we want to 'sell' ourselves to others, and get them to take a closer look at what's inside.

Other people may well pay more conscious attention to your 'packaging' than they do to some other elements of your total image. We know that clothing and grooming choices and decisions are made deliberately. We are aware that the fashion, cosmetics and food and health industries provide vast resources of information, products and services that we can buy to improve the way we look. Magazines and newspapers are full of advice on clothes and grooming.

To the critical eye, then, your clothing and grooming choices say a great deal about you. They indicate the nature of your self-image, how you see yourself and how you express your personality and values. That person with the critical eye may well know little about body language and voice and assume not much can be done to alter them. What he or she will realise is that, alongside the limitations imposed by nature, you will have made a number of conscious decisions about your appearance. To the critical eye, those decisions are significant.

Most people nowadays realise the importance of appearance. Contrary to what some people have thought in the past, especially in Britain, intelligence, ability and a smart appearance are compatible. Just consider how we *used* to regard a stereotypical academic, equating scruffiness with intelligence. I think our island status leads us to cherish eccentricity – in behaviour and dress. In America there is far greater emphasis on conformity.

The influence of America and Europe, and the increasingly international nature of business, have meant that the British have had to smarten up. You may think your appearance signals, 'My mind's on higher things', 'I'm too preoccupied to care about appearance', or 'Caring about the way I look threatens my masculinity', but you can't expect the critical eye to interpret those signals according to your meaning. Instead that critical person is likely to be thinking: 'He looks sloppy', 'She obviously doesn't have much self-regard', or worst of all, 'This person is insulting me and the situation by being so inappropriately dressed'.

Perhaps you are someone who looks good effortlessly, you have found your own style, and are never self-conscious about your appearance. Unlike more insecure individuals who are constantly titivating, adjusting their trousers or reapplying lipstick and checking how they look in any available reflective surface, you have your 'look' organised. You are confident about your appearance, and can get on with the job in hand. But what about the rest of us?

Many of us, with demanding jobs and families, have little time to spend thinking about details of appearance. In such a case it is useful to adopt a utilitarian approach, appreciating the importance of the subject and learning about how to make your appearance work effectively for you. Having done this learning and formulated some guidelines and habits, you can then get on with other things. You don't need to spend a lot of time on your appearance to look good, provided you have spent some time in thought and consideration of what suits you. You can regard your appearance as a necessary and powerful tool to help you achieve your goals.

For others among us, the 'shop till they drop' brigade, fashion and grooming are recreational activities, sources of relaxation. On one of my recent courses, a woman eloquently described her main leisure-time activity: whenever she needed a boost, she would go out without her credit cards or cheque book and with very little cash, and spend a couple of hours trying on *wonderful* clothes. The sight of herself in these outfits and the way they felt would give her an enormous boost. On returning from these trips, she would tackle her work with renewed vigour, fuelled by the incentive that one day she could be out there buying as well as trying the outfits.

In this chapter I will suggest some ideas to those of you who want to polish up your appearance but lack the guidelines. For those of you who are actively interested in the subject, I aim to add some further dimensions to the thoughts you have when you choose clothes and respond to the appearance of others.

MAINTENANCE: GROOMING AND UPKEEP

When someone has a 'maintained look' – clean, well-cut hair, clear skin, attractive teeth and hands – they exude self-esteem. We assume that someone who obviously cares for himself or herself is well-equipped to be responsible for others.

Like an effective exercise routine, good grooming depends upon establishing habits. And habits need to be repeated several times to stick. So if you decide to take action and regularly visit the dentist, hairdresser or manicurist, go armed with your diary and book appointments for the future. Even if you have to cancel a booking because something else comes up, you can change the date and ensure that you keep up the routine. When you start a new routine yourself at home, be it diet, exercise or grooming, make every effort to ensure that you start the routine as soon as possible after taking the decision. If you self-righteously carry out the new behaviour three times (notes and diary entries can help ensure that you do), there is greater likelihood of the habit sticking.

As regards consistency, it is important to be well-groomed and well-dressed every day at work. If you look good three or four days a week, but have a lapse for one day, people you work with may well take that as an indication of how you could behave in other respects. Perhaps you are not as reliable as they thought. There's always the likelihood, too, that on the very day that you forget to clean your shoes, or on the day *before* you go for that long overdue hair appointment, the managing director calls you in 'for a chat', or you have to lunch a new and important client.

Remember that your grooming habits are visible all the time. We often put great effort and attention into buying clothes that we will wear once a week, and forget to be meticulous about grooming.

Hair

Your hair should be cut every six or seven weeks. Find a good hairdresser who will advise you on style according to the shape of your face and type of hair, rather than one who replicates a standard 'salon style' that is currently in vogue. Your lifestyle should be taken into consideration and how much time and skill you have to do your hair yourself, in between visits to the salon.

Your hairstyle is a very important part of your total image. An old-fashioned hairstyle, particularly one that allows the hair to droop, pulling an observer's eye downwards, will be very ageing. A more modern style, with backward and upward direction, will lift the features. Our facial muscles succumb, like the rest of our bodies, to the pull of gravity as we get older, and so hair shapes that counteract 'droopiness' are more youthful. Short fringes do this effectively too, as they draw the eye of an observer upwards.

Your hairstyle can soften or sharpen your image. An abundance of curls and waves will emphasise rounded facial features and soft lines in your clothes; a sharp, geometric cut will emphasise chiselled faces and angular clothes shapes.

You will look less confident if you hide behind your hair, with long strands hanging over your face. Skinheads look aggressive because their hair is short, geometric and all their face is on display. A woman who has worn her hair long and full will find that more of an observer's attention is thrown on her make-up when she cuts her hair short, because there is less hair to fill up the picture. Large features can be balanced and made to appear less prominent by surrounding the face with a lot of volume of hair.

More women than men colour their hair, but it is accepted practice for both sexes. Techniques used by good hairdressers can be extremely subtle. Drastic changes in hair colour require a great deal of maintenance and you will need to pay a lot more attention to your clothes and, if you are a woman, your make-up. Eyelash and eyebrow tinting can be a useful and time-saving treatment for both sexes, and if you are careful, it is easy to do at home. It can draw attention to your eyes and give those with pale colouring a lot more definition to the features.

Some image consultants suggest that executive men look better clean-shaven. Certainly a beard or moustache can conceal a lot of the face, and prevent facial expression being 'read' effectively by others. Moustaches can suggest military values; while beards may be interpreted as an indication of rugged masculinity or a tendency to be 'off-beat'. To look well-groomed beards and moustaches should be kept clean, neat and regularly trimmed.

For a low-maintenance hair style, keep your hair as short as you can wear it (a good hairdresser will advise you), have it cut regularly, and use a combined shampoo and conditioner to wash your hair frequently.

Skin

Generally, women have finer, softer skin than men, so female skin needs more protection and nourishment. Both men and women need to clean their skin regularly and moisturise it, especially after exposure to the elements. Several leading skin care companies now offer complete ranges for men.

Although many people are still keen on getting a suntan, the ageing effects of exposure to the sun are now recognised. Some high factor suntan blocks are made especially for the face, and can be worn every day, even under make-up. Undoubtedly people look healthier with a tan; men and women can use bronzing powders (Guerlain make good ones for both sexes) to give themselves a healthy glow. Indeed, for women in a rush, with little time to put on foundation, a dash of bronzer and translucent face powder can quickly improve the look of the complexion. On television and in photographs, men and women can prevent shine on the face by applying translucent powder.

Nails

Hands are on display as much as your face, and need attention. Nails should be clean, shaped and regularly manicured. Zinc supplements can help weak nails to grow; but if you have problem nails or bite them, then it is worth going to a nail salon or talking to a manicurist. Durable 'tips' can be put on the nails which look extremely natural and protect your nails as they grow.

Teeth

Bad teeth may cause self-consciousness when smiling or even talking. Some people mumble because they are reluctant for others to see their teeth. It's worth investing in cosmetic dentistry if you need it; it can be very expensive but you'll enjoy smiling again. And unlike an expensive suit, your teeth are on display every day. Shop around for a dentist whose work is recommended and if necessary get a couple of 'quotes' for the work: dentists' fees can vary dramatically.

Perfume and After-Shave

More men need to wear effective deodorants and realise that underarm odour is *not* butch. (This assertion is made from personal experience on in-house company courses.) If you are working in close proximity to others, you don't want to become known as the person with the 'personal hygiene' problem. There are now environmentally friendly deodorants on the market that are extremely effective. So there really is no excuse.

Almost as intrusive to others is a perfume or after-shave that is overpoweringly strong. Our sense of smell is at its least acute in the morning and it is difficult to judge the impact on others. Wear a light, cologne-type perfume or after-shave during the working day, and save the strong signature smells for the evening.

Wardrobe Maintenance

Here are some tips:

- Avoid metal clothes hangers; they can damage shoulder lines.

- Hang clothes up immediately after wearing, and let them 'air' before putting away in a wardrobe to avoid creasing. Brush them if necessary before and after wearing.

- Don't expect to buy clothes that fit exactly; clothes are made in standard sizes, we are not. Find a good alterations person and get alterations done immediately. Good shops will often provide the service anyway.

- Dry cleaning shortens the life of clothes, and poor dry cleaning can ruin good fabric. Find a good dry cleaners and be prepared to pay a little more.

- Immediately repairs are needed, set the garment aside, rather than putting it back in the wardrobe or drawer and finding that you cannot wear it when you really need or want to.

- Scotchguard new shoes if they need it, and store shoes with shoe trees. Always find time to polish them. Many people consider scruffy shoes to be a bad reflection on the wearer.

- A routine helps to keep a wardrobe well-maintained. 'Police' your wardrobe once a week; go to the cleaners, polish shoes, get repairs done and check that your clothes are in order for the week ahead.

- When travelling, rolling rather than folding clothes and surrounding them in tissue paper or polythene can help reduce creasing. Hanging garments up in steam-filled bathrooms in hotels can help creases drop out.

EXPRESSING YOUR PERSONALITY

As we make conscious choices about our clothes, our dress can be regarded to reveal a great deal about personality. Earlier, in the second chapter of this book, I talked about introverts and extroverts. Dorothy Rowe in her study of this subject, *The Successful Self*, says that extroverts actively seek to stimulate others while introverts seek to distance themselves from too much stimulation. She goes on to say:

T hese notions of reducing or increasing stimulation underlie the actual choice of clothes. For some extroverts and introverts the choice is between 'dramatic' as against 'sophisticated'. For other extroverts it is between 'bright and colourful' as against 'cool and simple' or 'lots of jewellery, frills and scarves' as against 'plain and uncluttered'. Even amongst extroverts and introverts who don't care what they wear, this last distinction is important.

Does your style incline towards the extrovert or the introvert? You may find that you like lots of detail and like your appearance to attract attention and stimulate others, or you may prefer a simpler look which is not so obviously eye-catching.

The way we dress is again dependent on how much we wish to involve ourselves and identify with others, and how much we wish to distinguish ourselves and express our separateness. Some people seem to dress exclusively to shock and to provoke reaction; others merge into the background to such an extent that they are never memorable. Before we can look at how we express these conflicting needs in terms of clothes, I'd like to look at the three elements that give clothes their character – cut, cloth and colour.

Cut

The cut of a garment will be subject to the dictates of fashion, and the more extreme the cut, the more likely the garment is to date quickly. The cut determines how much yardage of fabric is used, how many pieces of fabric and how much detail there is in the garment.

For work, which for the majority of us is a structured activity with appointments and meetings, we tend to favour structured or tailored garments. For leisure time, by contrast, we choose unstructured, casual clothes like tracksuits and sweat-shirts.

The cut of a garment determines how much of our body shape is shown and how much it is disguised. Even a beanpole looks chunkier and squarer in square-shouldered box jackets and wide, baggy pants. Well-cut garments can often compensate for what we regard as faults.

As observers, we respond differently to specific shapes and assign various qualities to them. Curved shapes of collars, lapels and pockets will create a softer effect than strictly geometric shapes with lots of sharp angles. You can use these responses to dress appropriately for the situation – a plain, round-necked soft wool sweater making you seem relaxed and accessible, a sharply cut, tailored jacket suggesting authority and control.

The cut of a garment also determines how well it fits you. When you buy clothes you should always move in them as you will when you wear them. So if you are buying a jacket to wear at work, and you are constantly on the phone, it's worth checking that there is plenty of give at the elbows. If in doubt about fit, always go for the bigger size and have it altered, rather than wearing something that looks skimpy.

Avoid garments that are drenched in detail, with lots of obvious pockets, zips, elaborate collars and flashy buttons – unless, that is, you want your outfit to distract an onlooker from your appearance and message.

Cloth

The cloth of a garment will determine how warm it is, how quickly the garment creases and whether or not it needs to be dry cleaned. It will also affect how comfortable the garment is to wear; whether the cloth 'breathes' or not and how soft or stiff it feels.

Cloth and cut are interdependent. A closely fitting, tailored jacket would not work in a stiff bulky fabric like heavy velvet, and would be uncomfortable to wear.

Natural fibres – wool, cotton, linen – are most comfortable, though more expensive than many man-made fibres. Mixtures of man-made and natural fibres can be hard-wearing and do not crease so readily. Many suits today are made in cool wools which can be worn through most seasons apart from extremes in summer and winter. It makes sense in Britain to spend most on this weight of cloth, rather than splashing out on heavy tweed and very light summer-weights.

The cloth you wear creates associations for an observer, albeit uncon-scious ones. Take tweed, for instance. What associations do we make with this fabric? Rustic life maybe, conservatism possibly; we might conjure up a picture of the landowning gentry. Tweed is substantial and textured.

Now if we think of silk, we make some very different associations. We may think of sensuality, wealth and the exotic. Silk is soft, fluid and smooth. These associations affect how we choose garments and how we respond to them in others. You may go for tweed when you want to appear reliable, with traditional values; you may choose silk when you want a more urbane, affluent, sophisticated image.

Cloth that is smooth and shiny like satin, leather and sharkskin 'advances' towards the observer – as it is reflecting light it makes itself more prominent to the eye. Matt cloth, like tweed, suede and linen, 'retreats' because it absorbs more light.

Patterns also create associations. Remember how popular paisley was in the sixties? It still has 'arty' associations. For work, structured patterns with straight lines are popular; checks, stripes and tartans. Soft shapes with curved lines like polka dots and floral prints are more feminine. In blouses and ties these softer patterns can effectively balance the severity of a tailored suit. Unless you are very tall and striking-looking, large patterns worn over most of the body can overpower the wearer. Plain colours look better in photographs and on television. People should wear clothes, not vice versa.

Colour

Colour also has emotive associations. Warm, bright, light colours like red and yellow 'advance' and can make you appear friendly (wanting to stimulate others), while cool, sombre, dark colours, black, navy, grey, can 'retreat' and create distance, and make you seem more authoritative and powerful.

In urban areas, people favour the colours of the surroundings, grey, navy, black, stone and beige, while the traditional country colours are green and brown. In hot countries, dazzling sunshine drains away bright colour, so brilliant hues are more popular than in the more subdued light of northern cities.

Buying big items like suits and coats in neutral colours means that you do not tire of them quickly and they are versatile. Whole outfits of bright colours can easily overpower the wearer, particularly if he or she has delicate rather than dramatic colouring. The colour screams at other people and they overlook you. Dark neutrals make you look significant, while the warm neutrals, like beige, tan and camel, give more of a suggestion of approachability. These warm neutrals (possibly because they were the colours that the British wore in the colonies) also suggest 'class'.

The most important colour you wear is the one nearest your face. Blouses, shirts and ties should be in colours that suit and flatter your colouring. If you want to use colour to 'say' something then do it particularly in these items. Effective use of colour can make you look dynamic and confident; a lot of people are afraid of wearing strong colours. Make yourself look friendlier in a sharply tailored navy suit by wearing a warm brightly coloured polo shirt or blouse. Avoid a lot of wishy-washy pastel colours; at best they flatter a tan, at worst, they can look cheap and babyish.

ACCEPTABILITY

What you wear depends on where you work and your lifestyle. In some businesses like finance, accountancy and law, dress tends to be quite formal; in others like advertising, the media and fashion, there is a lot more leeway.

When appearances matter most, in interviews, presentations and meetings with new clients, remember the 'people like us' factor. If you are being interviewed to fit in with a company, you will need to look as though you blend in with the rest of the people who work there. When you are presenting a service you could offer a company, you need to look as though you can understand the values and needs of the company. You want to look as though you have something in common with your audience. If you work in advertising and your new client is a bank, then it would show respect and understanding to dress in a more formal way than the Levis and T-shirt that you might often wear to work. Whenever there is a high priority on working in a team, the more you look like the rest of the members the better.

The 'power dressing' uniform is well understood and copied, but these days people seem to have more difficulty with what I will call 'approachability dressing'. As director of a company, your navy pinstripe looks fine in the boardroom but could create division and distance when negotiating with union officials. You would be better off choosing a less severe mid-grey suit, or maybe the more relaxed look of trousers and a sports jacket. As a female manager who has to reprimand her team who have been working under enormous pressure, you could choose to leave your authoritative black suit at home and wear a softer, knitted, blue or green suit that makes you appear more understanding.

If you are seeking promotion, dress for the job you would like to be doing. This will make it much easier for those with power to visualise you in that position.

Men have fewer options when choosing clothes for work than women. The man's working 'uniform' of tailored jacket and trousers has seen few changes since Victorian times. It is easier for men to dress for acceptability. Women's clothes come in a wide variety of shapes and there is far greater choice. A garment can suggest overt romanticism, sexuality, domesticity or the exotic. Women have more scope to dress inappropriately for work. See the later section on Men and Women for further consideration of this.

INDIVIDUALITY

How, through clothes, do we balance our needs to conform and be accepted with the need to express our individuality? The extent to which you want to express individuality again depends on what you do. There is a very fine line between expressing that you are not particularly bothered by others' opinions of you and causing offence. As an entrepreneur going into a company to offer them some new, dynamic approach you can afford to express more individuality than if you were going in to integrate with and build a team from existing personnel.

Others can regard you as intrusive and insensitive if your dress is very loud and unconventional. Sometimes, dressing to scream for attention from others can seem like a compensation for inadequacies in your personality. It is possible to be acceptable to others and yet to 'dress for distinction'. Work out exactly what shapes and colours suit you, and what you feel comfortable in (see Suit Yourself, below) and then the values that you wish to suggest through your appearance. Distinguish yourself through clothes that look 'good'; that fit you well and are the best cut and cloth that you can afford. Someone who is effectively expressing individuality and has 'got the measure' of himself or herself will present a coherent total image.

You can use your image to express your individuality and reinforce what you do. For instance, if you deal with consumer complaints, you might want to emphasise approachability and reassurance by dressing in soft fabrics and warmish colours of medium intensity, rather than a sharp 'city slicker' suit. If you spend a lot of time presenting to large groups, you might want to emphasise your role as 'performer' by wearing bold colours and clothes with a touch of theatricality that do not compromise your professionalism.

Express individuality through unusual colours and attention to detail.

A dark green suit may be as appropriate for the job you do as the regulation navy that everyone else wears. Consider that when we communicate with one another we focus on the other person's face, head and shoulders; so women could express individuality through jewellery and scarves if they wear them, while men should choose shirt collars and ties especially carefully.

Bear in mind, too, that if you have to conform to dress standards at work, you always have your weekends and social life in which to indulge your taste for the exotic or the extreme.

It is easier for a woman to express individuality through the way she dresses. Many male executives tend to dress in 'airport lounge' style, buying ties, shirts and jackets at airports while waiting to depart. Better, instead, to visit a good department store and choose quality items that add distinction to your appearance.

The associations created by cut, cloth and colour convey values. You could show a *regard for tradition* through old school ties, pin-stripes, striped shirts, lovingly cherished leather briefcases and solid lace-up shoes, Burberrys and Barbours, William Morris print scarves, broderie anglaise blouses from Laura Ashley, kilts and antique watches. This is very much the 'British' style of dress. The American version is the 'preppy' look: loafers, button-down shirts, Brooks Brothers suits, prairie sweaters and denim coach bags.

This traditional look involves clear distinctions between colours for a 'town' or 'country' image. Your choice can suggest an 'outdoorsy' mentality or a more 'urban' orientation.

Japanese and European designers influence *a more modern look*. Chrome briefcases, designer watches, linen suits, the versatile beige jacket, distinctively cut clothes with bolder use of colour, and Italian shoes suggest greater awareness of modern design and fashion. Levis, plain white round-necked T-shirts and black leather biker jackets have become casual modern classics.

Duffel coats, round wire-rimmed glasses, dark thick tights, blazers and pleated skirts can lend the wearer *an academic air*. In strong contrast, you may choose to be flash or subtle to *convey your affluence*. Obviously expensive watches, blatant designer labels, acres of expensive leather and lots of gold set off with a deep suntan will indicate to others that you are proud of your financial success (this look is very popular in Florida). You may choose to display your wealth more discreetly through wearing low-key cashmere sweaters, quiet silk blouses and shirts, Levis with a real Rolex.

ACCESSORIES: ATTENTION TO DETAIL

A crisp white or pale blue shirt or blouse is a standard item in the working wardrobes of most people. It is commonly worn as interview dress under a smart suit. What does it indicate? To look good, a white shirt needs to be carefully laundered and ironed. Attention must be paid to the detail. It typifies the inferences that we make from clothes. If the wearer displays high standards and attention to detail in an item of clothing, then others assume the same qualities will be displayed at work.

At work, accessories are often functional. A briefcase literally 'packages' the results of your labours, a watch helps you regulate time. These accessories are thrown into prominence as they are used all the time. They will be noticed by others, so choose them with particular care. Too many accessories make people look cluttered and can be distracting. The person who carries a briefcase, portable phone and Psion organiser may come over as gadget mad; you want to make an impact for the way you perform, rather than be remembered for all the equipment you carried. Keep your accessories functional and effective – too many details like scarves and bits of jewellery can be distracting.

For women, matching accessories, shoes and handbags in light or bright colours, can look very contrived and ornamental rather than functional. Save them for weddings.

Choose spectacles with care. Like your hair, they are an element of your appearance that people see all the time. Buy a shape that flatters your face. You will emphasise a round, chubby face by choosing round frames – angular shapes would be more flattering. Avoid spectacles that make a strong statement in themselves, unless you want others to remember your glasses rather than your face. Take the advice of a good optician or a friend whose opinion you can trust.

SUIT YOURSELF: SHAPE AND COLOUR

Clothes can perform miracles in creating illusions with shape. The eye is attracted to detail and line, and so the cut you choose can accentuate parts of your body, or disguise them. The quality and texture of cloth, and colour, in that it 'advances' or 'retreats' to varying degrees, can make parts of you seem bigger or smaller.

Here are some suggestions for:

Tall People

Tall people can wear bolder, more dramatic clothes than small people. Baggy double-breasted jackets, full pleated trousers and billowing dresses and skirts can be carried off to effect.

With no need for streamlining, tall people can 'split' their bodies with blocks of colour and go for contrasting tops and bottoms. Checks and prominent patterns will not overpower the wearer.

You can carry off clothes made in fabrics with a lot of texture, like tweed, mohair and suede. Keep accessories bold and chunky too, and in proportion. A tall man or woman with a delicate little briefcase could look incongruous. To avoid looking gangly, pay attention to sleeve lengths, ensuring that the sleeve reaches the wristbone. Trouser and skirt lengths should also be long enough so that you look in proportion.

Short People

A short person can streamline his or her silhouette by choosing whole outfits in the same or toning shades. Suits are a better choice than strongly contrasting tops and bottoms. Men's shoes and socks can tone with their trousers, while if women choose shoes, tights and skirts in complementary colours they will appear taller. Trousers with turn-ups will 'shorten' the legs, while vertical creases along the length of trousers can help create a 'lengthening' effect. Vertical details like stripes, softly fitted darts, vertical seams help the illusion.

Single-breasted jackets are more flattering. Double-breasted jackets have horizontal detail in the buttons going across the body, which can make a person seem squarer. For women, shorter cropped jackets can make the lower half of the body seem longer, where a long jacket would dwarf it. Exaggeratedly high heels will draw attention to your lack of stature. Detail should be small and simple and kept to the top half of the body. Large, loose garments can swamp small people.

Smooth textures and neat patterns will maintain proportion. Large, bulky briefcases will emphasise, through comparison, your lack of stature. Billowing masses of hair can also overpower short people. Aim for an overall effect which makes you look compact.

Thin People

If you are thin, you can wear clothes with a lot of fullness, with gathers and pleats. Choose colours that 'advance' – warm, light shades, like creams and beiges. You can wear shiny fabrics that can make bodies seem larger. Garments with soft textures, like wools in preference to 'harder' finishes like gaberdines, will prevent you looking too severe.

Double-breasted jackets will add 'fullness'. Pockets and generously cut sleeves, wide trouser legs and full skirts can all fill you out. If you are very thin then avoid figure-hugging styles and choose a 'boxy' cut. Keep accessories in proportion and avoid heavy, chunky items.

Plump People

To look slimmer, choose clothes that are generously cut in matt, fluid fabrics rather than stiff fabric which will bulk you out. Choose single-breasted jackets and detail and patterns that create vertical lines – stripes, V-shaped necklines and inverted V-shaped jacket bottoms. Cool, dark colours will 'retreat' and make you seem slimmer. Keep pattern to small areas.

Tailored jackets that are gently fitted with darts can create an illusion that you have more of a waist than is actually there. For comfort's sake, choose elastic or part elastic waistbands. Men may find braces more flattering and comfortable than belts.

Draw attention away from your fat areas. Women can wear drop-waisted styles to camouflage a full stomach. With large hips, a woman can create balance in her silhouette by padding out her shoulders, so that her hips appear relatively smaller.

Camouflaging Certain Areas

The most flattering silhouette for everyone is one that attracts the eye of an onlooker upwards, towards the face. Most tailored clothes have padded shoulders and, as we associate well-shaped shoulders with responsibility and strength, we find this 'inverted triangle' shape more imposing. You don't need to pad your shoulders out like an American footballer, but square shoulders, whether formed by nature or by artifice, will make you look more authoritative.

You can create this 'inverted triangle' shape in other ways, too. Light colours worn on the top half of the body, will attract the eye upwards and make the top half seem bigger. Put texture, pattern, shine on the top part and smoothness, matt finishes and plain fabrics on the bottom to emphasise this shape.

Your Colouring

Image consultants pay a great deal of attention to choosing the right colours to bring out the best in your features. They suggest that we fall into certain categories, with predominantly light or dark, warm or cool, and muted or bright tones. The suggested colours you wear can be chosen according to whether your natural colouring is either predominantly blue- or yellow-based.

If you have sandy hair, brown eyes and freckled skin, you could choose to flatter that colouring by dressing in muted shades of brown, grey and tan, with gold, red and green as accent colours in blouses, shirts, ties and scarves. With more dramatic contrast in your colouring – black hair, pale skin and dark eyes – you may want to choose stronger contrasts of dark navy and white, with a clear red or turquoise as accent colours.

If you wish to read more about colour analysis, see the book list on page 190.

Be aware that some colours 'drain' light, others reflect it. If you wear black, khaki or beige near your face when you are tired, and you do not have clear, dramatic colouring, they may well make you look even more exhausted. Similarly, navy blue and purple can accentuate dark blueish shadows under the eyes. At such times, put white, ivory or creams near the face. These colours reflect light up on to the face of the wearer, and are immediately flattering.

MEN AND WOMEN: SOME CONSIDERATIONS

The changing status of women in the workplace has meant that both sexes have had to make adjustments to how they perceive one another. How is this reflected in dress?

Women have yet to break through what is known in America as 'the glass ceiling', the barrier between middle and top management. Although there is much less sexual discrimination today, women are in many cases still paid less than men, and are few and far between in key positions of power. Let us hope the imminent demographic changes will help rectify this. Discrimination, on the whole, tends to be maintained by gentlemen of 'a certain age', the 'old school'.

Even though discrimination against women is on the wane, many of us still hang on to strong values of what is masculine and what is feminine. Indeed, many of these values are to be preserved and cherished. Management education today recognises that an 'androgynous' approach is a most effective one: that is, understanding, appreciating and using the strengths of both masculinity and femininity. Lack of understanding of these values, particularly in the way they are expressed through clothes and presentation, can make it harder for men and women to work well together.

What do we associate with masculinity? Strength, power, the ability to lead, little show of emotion, toughness and grit. Role-models for men are strong, silent types; introverts who have strong, clear goals, are decisive and act upon their beliefs, regardless of what others may think. And these qualities are reflected in how we perceive men physically; it is easier to be a tall man in our society than a small one. It is hardly surprising that men have the 'uniform' they wear for work; masculinity emphasises action rather than presentation, and once a man has donned his uniform he can get on with the action.

In contrast, what associations do we make with femininity? Nurture, physical vulnerability, the ability to care, emotional expressiveness, soft-ness and smoothness. As men traditionally protect women, it is easier to be a small woman in our society than a very large one. Role-models for women are traditionally carers (Florence Nightingale, Helen Keller, Mother Teresa, Anita Roddick) or they are very beautiful. Presentation is important to women and many women have gained wealth and social standing through attracting and then marrying wealthy husbands.

Rather than 'strong silent types', women see themselves far more in terms of their relationships with others. They actively seek connection with others, like to talk about their feelings, and take on roles of wife, mother, hostess, as well as the role they adopt at work. Traditionally, women have been viewed to an extent as ornamental, and this function has affected their livelihood through marriage, so strong social conditioning has made them more interested in clothes and appearance. And because they have many different roles to play, and to dress for, they do not have quite the same established uniform for work that men do. In the seventies, though, many working women attempted to imitate the male uniform through 'power dressing'.

These notions of masculinity and femininity cause great discussion on courses. I train both single-sex and mixed groups and these are some of the views I've heard expressed:

'Women should wear exactly what they like and not compromise to fit in with men' (young woman).

'Women should not show too much flesh at work – most inappropriate' (older man).

'Men should pay far more attention to grooming – especially personal hygiene' (female manager).

'You can look far more relaxed with a group of women. I wouldn't necessarily wear a suit, I'd wear a sports jacket or even a sweater' (male manager).

'Why don't men look more interesting?' (middle-aged woman).

And my favourite, and one that came from a male senior executive in a multi-national company and bodes well for the future:

'What *do* women think about beards?'

Make of these what you will. How much you choose to adapt your clothing style for the people you are with will depend on your beliefs and personality. From my personal experience, I think that it is pragmatic to consider the values of people I am dealing with and to remember the 'people like us' factor. If you are of like mind, you may want to consider the following:

- Women tend to notice detail, men notice overall effect. For instance, a woman may notice that a man has an attractive tie, or a woman has used eye make-up well, whereas a man would think that the other man was dressed appropriately and the woman had a nice face.

- If you are prominent in a situation by virtue of your gender, then dressing to emphasise sexual stereotyping will increase that prominence. So the only woman on an otherwise all-male board of directors will emphasise her 'separateness' if she wears bright colours, flounces and frills, or lots of jewellery. This 'distinction' can work in her favour, indicating her self-possession and level of confidence. The most successful woman I know, who runs a company in the heavily male-dominated world of electronics, dresses to emphasise her femininity. She is already prominent and, rather than apologising for that in the way she dresses, she emphasises it. The only man on all-female board of directors will emphasise his 'maleness' if he dresses in traditional businessman's pin stripe, old school tie and stiff striped shirt. Again this may work well for him, if he wishes to create distance.

- If you want to play down your 'distinctiveness' then adapt *elements* of the other gender's clothing. Men can be extra careful with grooming and detail and soften up their uniform by wearing coloured waistcoats, sweaters under jackets, more colourful ties and shirts. Women can wear their most streamlined clothes, simple, tailored coat-dresses, skirts and contrasting jackets. There's more chance of looking like an 'imitation man' if you adapt too many elements; the classic navy blazer is more masculine than a shorter navy jacket with a rounded collar. Go for tailored clothes, but wear some of them in colours that mostly women tend to wear.

- Both men and women need to be aware of how body shape affects how masculine or feminine we look in clothes. Men are more angular than women, and sharply tailored clothes exaggerate masculinity. Softer tailoring or a sweater softens this effect. Women have rounded bodies, and a sweater will cling to contours and exaggerate them. Hence the femininity of twin-set and pearls, with rounding in both shape of garment and jewellery.

- It is sometimes said that a woman has to be twice as good as a man to get the same job. Men certainly need to know about a woman's achievements to accept her. You can use your appearance to help indicate achievement – having status-symbol accessories and dressing from international designers. Most men will sense quality from an Armani jacket, even if they don't recognise it as such. Slightly different considerations apply for a man wanting to be accepted by women. A woman boss will often be concerned that you and she understand one another and that you are not going to feel your masculinity is under siege by working for her. Women are quite often put off, I think, by men wearing obvious designer labels to suggest achievement, or flashy shiny suits, fake Gucci watches and gold chains.

- We equate power with size. A woman will exaggerate her femininity by wearing itsy-bitsy fine jewellery and too much light smooth shiny fabric. Choose jewellery and matt fabric that has more substance to appear less as though you need protection. Business dress for women is especially difficult in the summer. (In Britain men seem to wear virtually the same things all year round.) Wear safari colours rather than baby pinks and blues, and at work, unless you want to appear provocative, keep exposure of flesh limited.

- Finally, a personal bugbear. In business few men, even 'new men', seem to have mastered the technique of greeting women without giving us a quick 'once over' with the eyes. We welcome appreciation, but if when you greet us you could keep your eyes on our faces, rather than slyly scanning our anatomy, we would feel a lot more comfortable.

THE MINIMAL THOUGHT WARDROBE

These suggestions are *not* for people who like spending time shopping and thinking about clothes. They are for those of you who want to look good with minimum effort.

Create your own uniform according to the styles and colours that suit you. Make restrictions for yourself and stick to them. Base your wardrobe on two or three neutral colours that complement one another, black or navy, grey and white perhaps, or brown, beige and cream. Restrict bright colours in shirts, blouses and ties to one or two, as well. Limit the styles you wear and only buy clothes that fit in with these restrictions, especially in sales. In the working wardrobe a man could limit himself to single-breasted suits, button-down shirts, lace-ups and striped ties, for instance; a woman could limit herself to short jackets, straight skirts, gold jewellery, plain court shoes. Your casual 'uniform' could be tracksuits or denim jeans and a jacket.

Find a designer or shop that suits you and only shop there. Plan two major shopping trips a year, in early spring and early autumn when shops are full of new stock.

Alternatively, if you have one outfit on which you would like to base your uniform, find someone who can make your clothes according to your specifications. You won't need to waste time looking around the shops at all then, but you will have to go for fittings.

People in public life often have distinctive 'uniforms'. Margaret Thatcher for instance, wears round-necked plain suits for business and at social events. She wears the same *shape* of clothes to social functions, only the fabric tends to be more appropriate for evening (this is a useful guideline for how to dress when socialising is connected with business – keep shape the same but vary fabric). The restrictions of style make her image distinctive.

Ronald Reagan also had a 'uniform'. On formal occasions, he always wore very powerful, dark, large formal suits, that emphasised his stature. On holiday he was 'costumed' in distinctive cowboy-style clothes that still made him look larger than life. The British politician David Steel always wears dark or striped shirts with white collars, a look that has old-fashioned, upper-class connotations and which makes him eminently distinctive.

Showbusiness people also wear 'uniforms'. Cher is renowned for her outrageous Bob Mackie dresses, while Bruce Springsteen wears jeans, T-shirts and muscle. Were Cher suddenly to start wearing Ralph Lauren, or Bruce Springsteen tailored business suits, fans would find the change of image confusing.

If you find your own style for your 'uniform' you will undoubtedly present a consistent and distinctive total image. Accessories can be used to suit the occasion or reflect your mood.

THE MINIMAL COST WARDROBE

To dress well for little money you need to remember the 'cost per wear' theory. The value of a garment can be estimated by its cost divided by the number of times you wear it. So a £40 jacket that you wear once works out a lot more expensive than a £200 jacket that you wear a hundred times.

Remember that dry cleaning requirements need to be taken into consideration when you buy a garment, and add to the effective cost. Check that the garment really does require dry cleaning – sometimes it is just stipulated to protect the manufacturer. I've washed shirts that say 'dry clean only' and have been pleased with the results.

Familiarise yourself with where you would like to buy clothes if you could afford it. Get to know the stock and try it on, then on the first day of the sale you can get there early and buy without trying on. Avoid purchases that are that season's colour, stick to safe neutrals. Buy small items for flashes of colour.

Always buy clothes cut on the generous side. Skimpy clothes look cheap. Designer sales and nearly-new shops can be good hunting grounds. Some looks, like a traditional image, an outdoors image or academic image, are easier to achieve with less money.

Cheap clothes will be overlooked if you have expensive, good-quality accessories. Buy the best shoes and briefcase you can afford, and relate them to your hair colour. After all, you wear your hair colour all the time, and matching your shoes and briefcase will create a coherent image.

Spend money on whatever you are seen in most. If you are meeting people outside, your coat should be your major investment. Otherwise, spend as much as you can on a good jacket, and wear it over cheaper shirts, blouses, skirts and trousers.

If you are in that sort of business, procure a fake expensive watch. From a distance no one will know the difference. Get your hair cut regularly at the top hairdressing schools. Good grooming can compensate for non-designer clothes. You can look good on a limited budget. Be selective and plan your purchases carefully. Never buy on impulse because it was 'cheap'. Go for a more classic look, rather than slavishly following fashion, and vary your look by buying more of smaller items, distinctively different shirts and blouses to change the appearance of a suit.

chapter six

YOUR VOICE AND SPEECH

S omeone once called the voice 'the second face' and indeed our voices reveal our history almost as much as our faces do. Very often, though, in work on self-presentation, voice and speech get overlooked. We forget that when we make a first impression the initial impact is visual, then, when we start to speak, the impact of voice and speech takes over. In terms of developing a total image, voice is frequently a 'poor relation'. Why do we overlook the voice in this way?

We are generally more aware of what we see than what we hear. Though some people are particularly responsive to sound, most of us do not hear, or more significantly listen, to anywhere near the extent that we could. We are bombarded these days by the visual image. For instance, it is as much the video (what we see) that sells a pop record as the music itself (what we hear).

We are surrounded by information that is conveyed through visual means, from computer screens, ever-thicker newspapers and advertising hoardings. Even what could be classed as mainly 'aural' media, the radio and telephone, need visual support. For many of us, the radio serves to provide a meaningless drone in the background or a diversion during traffic jams. Most personalities who become popular on the radio seek television exposure to build on their celebrity. On TV they reach a wider, more receptive audience. On the telephone, so far, it is of course the speaker's voice that really matters, but it could diminish in importance. Tele-communications experts have already developed the prototype of the video phone, a telephone which is video linked so that you can see the caller. If this technology becomes available for popular use, phone calls, too, will involve as much visual as aural response.

Most of us who live in cities are used to a certain background noise (traffic, tube trains, sirens) twenty-four hours a day. When we visit the countryside we suddenly hear specific sounds again, birdsong, insects buzzing, grass rustling. It often seems shockingly quiet. In most offices there is a continuous background drone of central heating, air conditioning, elevators and telephones. We get used to this sound environment and are rarely conscious of it. However, the background buzz desensitises us to other sounds and makes us less receptive to them.

In the hairdresser's, supermarket, airport, taxi, we are surrounded by piped music which we barely notice. This continuous onslaught of sound dulls our hearing and listening skills and, unless we make a conscious effort to do otherwise, we lose the capacity to appreciate and interpret the sound of the human voice.

In this country there is great sensitivity about the way people speak. I quote from an American book: 'In Britain, the accent, intonation, use of vocabulary, even the length of sentences bespeak one's birth and position – much more so than clothing or body language.' This certainly was the case and we are still probably the most accent-conscious country in the world. Many of us, if we are honest, dislike certain British accents more than others, or we may suspect that we have an accent that others hold prejudice against. Like all 'delicate' subjects, we tend to think that if we ignore the problem area, it will go away. This is why we often choose to disregard the voice as an important part of self-presentation. So, ironically, we choose to ignore the voice because we know that significant judgements are made about it and that perhaps some of these judgements are unreasonably bigoted.

Accent aside, your voice is very personal. Your voice is linked to the way you feel about yourself, and criticism of your voice feels like an attack on your personality. Let's consider what your voice can 'say'.

WHAT YOUR VOICE 'SAYS' ABOUT YOU

Your voice can indicate how you are feeling, how relaxed and healthy you are, where you are from, your education, how much you adapt to peer group pressure. Your voice reveals your psychological 'history'; many an individual who mumbled because of shyness and self-consciousness in their teens has retained the habit into adulthood. And again, like other aspects of our total image, we use our voices to fit in with others or to assert our individuality. Women working in a dominantly male culture, for instance, will sometimes pitch their voices lower than is natural for them, because they want to fit in (and often this adjustment will be made unconsciously). On the other hand, someone who moves to London from another part of

Britain might stubbornly cling to a distinctive accent in order to assert a sense of regional identity.

Your voice and speech are absolutely unique to you, as individual as your fingerprints. It is your sound, a way of saying 'I am', and it makes a substantial impact on others. If your self-esteem is low, you'll show it through your voice. Your voice is more powerful than a musical instrument. Not only can it evoke and express emotion, tell someone 'I love you', make people laugh, but it can also persuade juries of your innocence, incite the masses to vote for you, help you win a job interview or get that sales contract. You cannot hear your voice in the way others hear it, because you receive the sound through bone conduction in your head. You can, however, develop sensitivity to and awareness of your voice and its impact on others.

Your voice is a vital part of your total image. We all know instances of people whose appearance and voice seem incompatible; the large woman with the breathy, helpless tone, the small man with the booming bass notes. When people first meet you they make judgements about you based on what they see and then they seek confirmation of these decisions through what they hear. The sound of your voice should reinforce the impact of your appearance. Lazy, sloppy speech is as detrimental to your image as poor grooming. Most of us can recollect an occasion when we have met someone new, liked the way they look and then felt let down when they opened their mouths.

In business today, telephone skills are extremely important. Many of us use the phone a great deal to establish initial contact with others. The more you use the phone, the more important it is to develop good voice control. You are making that vital first impression through your voice alone, and when you eventually meet the person at the other end, they will have formed a clear image of you. Indeed, a pleasant voice can make an individual a lot more attractive and can often compensate for a rather ordinary appearance. Many public figures in politics and show-business have worked on their appearances to match naturally good voices, or taken voice and speech training to complement their good looks. Some celebrities even capitalise on voices that are not especially pleasant on the ears, that at best could be described as distinctive. Derek Jameson and Janet Street Porter, for example, make their voices their unmistakable trademarks. Their sound, although not necessarily considered pleasing, is a vital, significant part of their public images.

You are less likely to be interrupted and cut short in meetings, or on the phone, if others like listening to the sound of your voice. You have a 'speaking image' and you owe it to yourself to make the best of it.

CAN VOICES BE CHANGED?

One of the reasons why people do not like to try to improve their voices is because they suspect that little can be done about them. They believe that a strident pitch or a breathy tone is something that they're born with and that they have to put up with. Also, the workings of the voice seem somewhat mysterious and anatomical. If you go to an exercise class often enough, you can see the improvements in your shape; you can only hear the fuller tones of your voice and see the results at one remove, in the reactions of others. In improving your voice you are more dependent on the feedback of others.

You can dramatically alter the way you use your voice, by learning how the voice works and doing exercises to improve its production. There are very few people who cannot benefit from voice work, in the same way that most of us can benefit from exercise, or learning about body language, or by taking up a regular grooming routine. Many actors use voice work to maintain their voices in a strong, receptive and versatile condition.

When a voice is receptive, it is under your control, and it will be responsive to your emotions. Voices sometimes get 'blocked', and the way the voice is produced will prevent it expressing a range of feelings. We hear this in voices that always sound miserable, or 'intellectual' and objective, or that have a permanent forced cheerfulness in the tone.

Even though your personality conditions the way you sound (you could be shy, for example, and so you talk in a quiet voice to avoid attention), you can learn through *physical* means to produce a fuller voice. This will change the way other people regard and react to you and, in turn, the way you feel about yourself. Of course, if your shyness is causing you anxiety, then you may need help on a psychological level, but you can help your shy *behaviour* through physical work on the voice.

So though there is a strong psychological influence over the way you use your voice, essentially voice is produced in the body and it does not work in isolation from the other parts. Although I have stressed the auditory impact of the voice, we can also 'see' the voice working. Voice and body language often work together and reinforce each other. When you look at someone with a quiet voice you can see that they are breathing in a shallow manner, and that they are not opening their mouth and using their facial muscles as much as they could. The shy speaker could also look downwards and avoid eye contact. The more you become aware of the physical nature of voice production, the more you can improve the power, versatility and control of your own voice.

Many of you are vocal athletes, speaking at length each day on the phone, or in presentations or meetings. Perhaps you have to use your voice a lot in competition with background sound. You can train your body to produce good sound in these situations, in the way that an athlete can train his or her body to run a marathon. You can help save your voice from feeling and sounding tired. By doing the suggested exercises regularly for a few minutes each day, you can develop your voice to become one of the best assets of your total image.

THE DIFFERENCE BETWEEN VOICE AND SPEECH

People often get confused between voice and speech. Old-fashioned elocution teachers often taught their pupils how to speak 'correctly' with little attention to voice production.

Speech is formed by the actions of the speech organs on the sound produced by the voice. Many 'speech' problems disappear when voice production is improved. Today, the emphasis in voice and speech training is on the development of the potential in the natural voice, rather than training people to speak in an artificially imposed manner. This chapter includes exercises for both voice and speech.

EFFECTIVE BREATHING

In Chapter Four, the importance of good posture in sending out the best sort of visual signals was stressed. Posture is also fundamentally important for effective voice production. Poor posture can cause constriction of the ribs and lungs, reducing the space available for breath. As mentioned earlier, postural 'quirks' are often caused by tension spots in the body, and tension travels very quickly. Just clench your fist tightly again for a moment, and feel the muscles at the top of your arm tense. As you continue to tense your fist, your jaw muscles will also feel locked – and this will affect voice production.

Similarly, it is a short journey for tension to travel from the shoulders or back of neck to the muscles in the front of the throat around the voicebox, the larynx. This tension can effectively 'strangle' your sound. All the exercises prescribed in this chapter should be done after first checking that your posture is working to your advantage. Check for tension by gently nodding the head up and down and from side to side and gently rolling the shoulders back and forward to ease out any bunched muscles.

Along with posture, the other governing factor over the sound that you produce is the way you breathe. These two aspects of your physical 'use' affect not only your sound, but the way that you control stress in your body. In a fascinating book called *Body and Personality*, Brian Wells examines the many ways of controlling stress and concludes, 'In each case, breath control is basic; it is the one element which most clearly typifies virtually every attempt, Eastern or Western, to achieve mental goals through physical practices. Postural control is a close runner up.'

Breath is the energy that produces voice, and without good breath control you cannot hope to have a powerful voice. We produce voice by the breath vibrating on the vocal chords in the larynx. If breathing is strained and effortful, as it is in many of us under stress, then obviously the voice suffers. So before I look at the direct link between breathing and voice production, I would like to consider how stress and breath affect one another.

Stress and Breath

Under stress, your breathing pattern will change. When we feel under pressure we tend to overbreathe, taking in too much oxygen and expelling too much carbon dioxide. We breathe in quickly and in the upper part of the chest. Intakes of breath are audible, rapid, frequent and snatched. The chemical balance of the blood, which is dependent upon controlled amounts of oxygen and carbon dioxide, goes haywire. At worst we hyper-ventilate – our chests feel tight, hearts seem to flutter and we feel light-headed. We feel as though we are experiencing a panic attack.

This breathing, which is called clavicular breathing (after the collar bone, the clavicle), forms a vicious circle with the mind. We associate feeling panicky and out of control with effort in breathing in, so we snatch in the breath. The brain, via the chemical imbalance in the blood, then gets a message from the body of physical panic, confirming what it suspects. It sends more messages back to the body, perpetuating the panicky condition.

Babies, unaffected by psychological and physical inhibition, have fantastically powerful voices (as those of you who are parents will know). If you watch a baby breathing, you will see that it releases its stomach out as it breathes in. It is breathing in the bottom part of the lungs, which have most capacity. The lungs are pear-shaped, and the base of the lungs is protected by the bottom of the rib cage, not far about the waist. Below the lungs is a sheet of muscle called the diaphragm, which drops down

101

when the lungs fill, letting the stomach muscles release out. Breathe IN, stomach OUT. On expiration, the diaphragm rises and the stomach muscles drop down. Breathe OUT, stomach IN.

This is the reverse of what many of us expect to happen when we take in breath. We expect to make an effortful movement of the chest, so that it puffs out. Breathing in this manner, using only the upper part of the chest, wastes an enormous amount of energy and breath capacity in the lungs. Both sexes can use this unnecessary chest movement and it can easily become habitual.

Hyper-tense individuals will breathe in this way a great deal of the time, making themselves feel panicky and getting easily tired. Researchers in West London discovered that hyperventilation was contributing to and perhaps even causing ME, the debilitating post-viral syndrome which can exhaust people for several years. The doctors arranged for their patients to have breathing lessons to break the hyperventilating habit.

One of the gravest misconceptions about breathing is that we are conditioned to think that when we go into a difficult situation we should take a deep breath IN. Usually, the level of physical tension being at the level it is, we then tend to hold our breath. If I am going to do something requiring physical exertion this could cause strain. If I go to lift a heavy table for example, take a breath and hold it tight in the upper part of the body, then the top part of my body, including my back, is expanded and tense. I am far more likely to strain or pull a muscle or tendon, with the combined pressure of the lifting effort and the tension of holding the breath. I would lessen the likelihood of strain by releasing the breath out as I lifted.

When we speak while holding the breath, the sound is first constricted and then it tails off in a tumble of weak-sounding words as the held breath is rapidly expelled. To control your breathing and response to stress, it is therefore the OUTbreath that requires control. This applies to physical and mental exertion, and is the way to control the breath during hard aerobic exercise. In a state of complete panic, if you can think of nothing else, think of controlling your OUTbreath by consciously blowing OUT and your breathing pattern will settle, thereby regulating your carbon dioxide and oxygen levels and helping your panic subside. (The age-old remedy for panic attacks and hysteria was to get the sufferer to stick their head in a paper bag so that they rebreathed in the carbon dioxide they had expelled, and thereby adjusted the balance.)

Unless you have something physiologically wrong with you, then breathing in should be effortless. The ribs swing out automatically, drawing air into the sponge-like lungs. The breath just drops into the available space in the body, and then the muscles that control the movement of the ribs control the expiration. If you breathe using the stomach, then you are making economic use of your energy, as you are not wasting energy expanding parts of the body which do not have space to hold the breath. The amount of breath that you have available for use will be eight to ten times as much as if you were breathing in a clavicular manner. So you are getting more breath for less effort, a good deal all round.

Those of you who had asthma or other breathing difficulties as children have more cause to associate stress with effort in breathing. You could well have a psychological 'memory' of this, and even though your medical problems have cleared your instinctive response to panic might be to start gasping. Some of you, particularly the weight-conscious, may find it difficult to release the stomach muscles to let the breath drop deep into the body because you habitually clench in your stomach and tense the muscles in an attempt to make it flatter. However, the way to get a flatter stomach is through exercise and diet, rather than by keeping it permanently tense. On the plus side, though, by breathing with the tummy you do effectively tone up those flabby muscles.

Poor breath control, then, is characterised by hearing sharp, short intakes of breath and seeing excessive unnecessary movement in the shoulders and chest on inspiration. This breathing pattern also influences the effect of speech, as we shall see later. People who use this breathing when they are communicating with others cannot exude confidence. Though 'observers' are unlikely to interpret these signals consciously, they will see obvious physical effort in the movement of chest and shoulders, and hear the speech flow fractured by audible 'gasps' for air. In miniature, these are the symptoms of hysteria. Using this sort of breathing is very tiring and makes an observer sense that you are nervous, tense and needing to make a great deal of effort.

Exercises for Breathing to Control Stress

These exercises can help you if you:

- feel panicky often.

- get breathless easily when under stress.

- rush to try and please everyone at the expense of your self-possession when you are talking.

- feel out of control when you are put on the spot.

1. Look in the mirror and take in a breath. Do your shoulders and chest rise? Can you hear the breath being sucked in? Do you ever recognise this experience? Lie on the floor, sensing your back and neck spreading and lengthening on the floor. Bend your knees up so that your feet are flat on the floor, but not so close to your bottom that the small of the back curves away from the floor. Put a book or cushion under the head to follow the natural curve of the spine. Check that your neck and shoulders are tension-free. Place a hand on your stomach, around about your navel and sigh and yawn out. (Sighs and yawns are the body's instinctive response to releasing tension, by expelling breath and slowing down the breathing. Smoking, to an extent, does the same thing, in that it slows down the outbreath.)

   Sense that the sighs and yawns are coming from your stomach and that the stomach is collapsing as you let the sound out.

2. Still lying down, pant gently while keeping the hand on the stomach; you should sense some movement. Do not do this for too long as it is very tiring, just long enough to sense movement of the diaphragm.

3. Still on the floor, have a good belly laugh, literally. With your hand on the diaphragm, you should sense some movement in the stomach.

4. In the same position, breathe in, feeling the stomach rise, and sensing it drop as you gently blow out the breath. Sense that when you have exhaled you do not immediately need to inhale. Indeed, you may be able to sense your ribs swinging open after exhalation, creating space for the breath to drop in to the body. This pausing for a moment in between breaths can really slow your rate of breathing down and be very relaxing. Even when you have exhaled as much as you possibly can, the lungs still hold a considerable amount of air.

5. Breathe easily (do not try and increase your intake of oxygen during these exercises) while keeping aware of stomach movement and breathe out while saying a word like 'relax' or 'rest' or 'let go' – whatever you feel appropriate.

6. Move to a sitting position, and monitor your breathing. If your chest has started to rise then place one hand on it, to remind it to settle. Repeat the exercise that you found most useful from 1–5 above, in this sitting position.

7. Stand in front of the mirror and do exercise 5. Check that you are not physically tense, that your shoulders are dropped and that your chest is not rising. Look at your face to see if you are tense, if your brow is

furrowed with concentration. Remember: these are breathing exercises and you have been breathing all your life.

Note

During these exercises, if you start to feel dizzy or light-headed at any time then stop. It is likely that you have upped your oxygen intake too much and surprised your brain. Return to breathing as you normally do, and focus on the outbreath. If you notice points of physical tension during these exercises, then refer to Chapter Four for exercises to relax specific areas.

With a partner (these exercises help check the panic response):

8. Play interrogators, with partner A firing questions at partner B. The questions can be of as personal and probing a nature as A likes; B does not have to respond with the truth. When B receives a question, he or she (with hand on stomach if it helps) consciously breathes in, then starts to breathe out and then speaks. There will be an unnaturally long time between B receiving and answering the question, during which A will look for evidence of clavicular breathing and (from Chapter Four) any evidence of the 'flight or fight' response. Partners then swap functions. The objective of the exercise is for B consciously to use breathing to control any panic reactions. Very useful as a pre-interview exercise.

9. This exercise is the equivalent of being in front of a talking 'firing line'. A fires topics at B, who must start talking straightaway (after he or she has consciously used breathing in and out to control the panic response and has checked that he or she is using the stomach for breathing). B is not allowed to stall for time by commenting on the topic (eg holidays, um, yes, that's an interesting matter, my gosh, what shall I say about holidays). When A feels like it, he or she can hurl another topic, the more surprising the better. Do not allow B to get into a predictable rhythm, whereby they know they are going to get about two sentences out before you throw them another topic. Keep surprising them. Then swap. It is important not to worry about the content, just to keep watching out for disrupted breathing and panic responses.

Breath and Speech

We use the outbreath to provide the energy for sound: we need to pause when we breathe in, then as we breathe out we speak. As clavicular breathing is characterised by short, frequent intakes of breath, it follows that this sort of breathing chops up the flow of speech into short phrases. When the breathing is working well, body and mind work together, and we take breaths where there are natural breaks in the content, where the 'punctuation marks' would occur in the sense of what we are saying. If your speech style is choppy, with short phrases, it will convey a different impression from a more fluent, smoother rhythm. Fractured sentences are not as easy to listen to, and you will not seem confident and in control. You are also far more likely to be interrupted, because your speech flow is broken by lots of short pauses that allow others to intervene. Contrast the two following patterns:

Speech flow ____ ____ ____ ____ ____

Here there are lots of short gaps for interruption.

Speech flow _____ _____ _____

With longer and less frequent pauses, the speaker can keep talking for a sustained time, cutting down the number of opportunities for interruptions.

When we are frightened our voices sound 'wobbly'. That is because our breathing has become shallow and jerky, rather than coming out in a steady stream. If the breath is not coming out of the body in a sustained, controlled way, then your speaking style can be characterised by a 'tailing off' in energy level at the end of sentences. You will not appear definite or resolved in what you are saying and you could come over as half-hearted and apologetic. The intention in what you are saying will not carry through to the end, so if you are trying to assert yourself, your manner of speaking will not help. You start speaking with a great gust of breath leaving the body and then there is insufficient left to sustain you to the end of your phrase. Do the exercises in this section to help you. Remember these exercises when you are in a 'wobbly' situation, and your voice will not give you away!

A breathy tone of voice is often considered sexy, probably because it reminds us of love-making; and certainly that association helped Marilyn Monroe build her image. Breathy voices sound as though there is very little breath control and the impression created can be weak, vulnerable and, in women, 'little girly' – great over a candlelit dinner for two, but not very effective if you are making a sales presentation or chairing a meeting. Though breathy speakers can be effective in an intimate medium, when they need to project their voices, they can have problems. The breath provides the power and support for the voice, and their breath control will be inadequate.

Getting good sound out of a voice when the breath is not working well is like trying to get a fire going without any oxygen. People who are not using their breath to support the voice often compensate in other ways to create a bigger sound. They may tense in the throat, mistakenly thinking that they can produce a bigger voice that way, and the tone will sound strident. They may raise the pitch, thinking that this will give the voice more power. They could even start to use exaggerated movements of the head, and gesticulate wildly in a mistaken attempt to 'enlarge' their communication. Many pitfalls in speaking arise because people do not trust the breath to provide power, and so they over-compensate in a destructive way in another part of the body.

Exercises to Connect Breath and Speech

These exercises differ from the ones in the previous section, in that they focus on developing control of the outbreath to sustain sound. It is import-ant to do the above exercises first, to get the breathing working and to avoid the bad habits caused by a reaction to stress.

Do these exercises if:

- you would like to sustain sound longer when you speak and sound more assertive, less 'wobbly' in certain situations.

- a breathy tone is making you sound younger than you would wish to.

- you wish to make your voice more powerful.

- you think that you 'push' your voice, in the throat, or by raising the pitch.

- you are an excitable speaker and get breathless when talking.

- you lose your place when you are speaking and forget what you are going to say next.

- you sense that people do not feel at ease listening to you.

1. When you feel that you are breathing naturally from the stomach, then do these exercises sitting or standing. With a hand on the abdomen, let the breath drop in to the body and then breathe out for 1, take another easy breathe and breath out while counting to 2 and continue to build up the count for the outbreath to about 10, provided you feel no

discomfort. Count aloud. Place your hands on your front ribs and sense how they swing in and out when you breathe. Check that your shoulders have not risen and that they are relaxed. The ribs and abdomen provide a large, powerful 'girdle' to support the breath. Breathe in freely and build up your count on the outbreath from 1 to 10, sensing the ribs control the breath in a steady stream as they descend. Put your hands on your back ribs (again, check the shoulders are dropped) and see if you can sense some movement there. You could be surprised at how large an area the back ribs protect. There is a great deal of space in there for the breath, and professional voice users who have exercised for years will have worked the rib muscles so that the back ribs swing wide apart to utilise that space.

2. Breathe out while making sound, sighing and yawning, let the pitch drop at the end of the phrase but maintain the intensity of the sound. If it is still dying away, then use a physical gesture, like pushing the arm away from the body, to help keep the energy going. Take a sentence, 'The breath sustains the sound to the end of the phrase,' and do exactly that. Check that posture is easy and that breathing is low in the body.

3. This exercise requires you to run a commentary on how you use pause to breathe. Many people have found it extremely useful in making them aware of their individual breathing patterns, in learning to control the breath, to create fluent speech and in helping to keep the brakes on the pace.

a   Take a mundane subject, like what you have done so far on a particular day.

b   Talk about this subject, and every time before you need to pause for breath, slip in the phrase 'I pause and I breathe'. Say it aloud.

c   Do not concern yourself with your content, what you are saying, that is unimportant. Just make sure that every time you need to breathe, you precede the pause with the phrase 'I pause and I breathe'. You will need to premeditate slightly when you are going to take these pauses. Then take time to let the breath drop low to the bottom of the lungs.

d   If it is helpful to you, keep a hand on your stomach to remind you to breathe 'low'.

e   Repeat the exercise, but this time *think* 'I pause and I breathe', rather than saying it aloud.

f   Do this exercise with a partner or a tape recorder.

Note: Several things can happen in this exercise. If you tend to snatch breath then you will want to gasp some in before you say 'I pause and I breathe' rather than after. You could find, because you have suddenly become aware of your breathing, that you need to breathe very frequently. Keep doing the exercise until you feel comfortable taking sufficient breath in the pauses to keep you going over several phrases. Remember that the breathing and breaks in the sense of the content should come together. The objective of this exercise is to make you aware of how you speak and the fundamental nature of breathing in this process. Let the exercise happen, rather than trying too hard to get it 'right' and thereby inducing tension.

Better Breathing

When we speak, we breathe in through our mouths and out through our mouths. When we sleep, we usually breathe in through our noses and out through our mouths. Wind instrument players have sometimes learned 'circular breathing' and they might retain the habit of breathing in through the nose and out through the mouth simultaneously.

Effective use of breathing can affect everything you do. Oxygen is the life force of our bodies, and if we receive it in ample, steady amounts, it can only make us feel better. Through consciously altering your breathing pattern you can calm yourself down. By building good breathing habits, you can ensure that your voice is strong and always sounds controlled. Steady breathing can help you deal with physical and mental exertion and fatigue. Yoga, meditation, stress control courses and the martial arts all place some emphasis on breath control. If you play sport of any description, then by paying attention to your breathing, breathing OUT through the effort and letting the breath drop in low in the body, you will improve your performance.

PACE AND PAUSE

People who talk very quickly often do not give themselves time to get adequate breath. Pace is all about the use of pause. A rapid rate of delivery is fine, provided the words are clearly enunciated and pauses are long enough for others to assimilate what you have said. Someone who speaks with a slow rate of delivery and fails to use pause will be deadly boring.

You need to pause to let the breath drop into the body, so that there is a fuel recharge, to let the brain organise the content before you speak, and to let others assimilate what has been said. Pauses provide mini-'rests' for mind and body.

To pause in conversation is also polite and considerate; it conveys the impression that there is space for the other person to chip in, should they want to. Pauses also allow you to check how the message you are sending is being received by the other person. There is an interesting cultural difference here, in that generally the British hold pauses slightly longer than Americans. This could contribute to the widely held British view that Americans are overpowering and verbose. An American will say something, pause for x seconds waiting for a response, then if nothing happens, will pick up the thread of conversation. Meanwhile the British person, whose pauses are x + y seconds, will be just about to speak when the American is off and running with the conversation again.

Why don't many of us make sufficient use of pause? Rapid pace can be the sign of a very quick mind. Unfortunately, there is no point in having a mind like quicksilver and a tongue to match, if you express your ideas so rapidly that nobody can follow them. Many of us talk quickly because of nerves, and the clavicular style of breathing that we force ourselves into perpetuates that state. We want to get things over with, to get the focus of attention away from us, so we rush. We could think that we are boring or not worthy of attention, and so we express things at a rapid pace which, ironically, makes the way we speak even more tedious and difficult to follow.

Some of us don't trust ourselves to hold pauses and so we fill them with 'ums', 'ers', throat-clearing, 'you knows', 'I means', lip-smacking, clicks of the tongue. Short 'ums' and 'ers' make us sound indecisive, lacking in confidence and hesitant. Longer 'ums' and 'ers' make us sound arrogant and pompous; we are keeping everyone else hanging around while we do our thinking aloud.

In terms of establishing trust, these mannerisms are counter-productive: ums and ers, for instance, increase when people are lying. A confident speaker does not need to fill in pauses with these sounds or qualify what he or she is saying by lots of 'I means' and 'you knows'. Unnecessary sound mannerisms detract from our message and act as barriers to communication.

If you feel comfortable making effective use of pause, you do a great deal for your total image. People will feel relaxed and at ease with you, because you seem to be at ease with yourself. It is a sign of great confidence to be able to pause and do nothing, the 'speaking' equivalent of being able to stand and sit still. It reassures others to see and hear that you are pausing to think as you speak, and because of this you will convey authority.

Exercises for Making Better Use of Pause

Do these exercises if you:

- gabble.

- go blank when you are talking.

- um and er a lot.

- are always being asked to repeat yourself (which can be very undermining).

1. The 'I pause and I breathe' exercise in the previous section will help you. It is very difficult to monitor your own speaking pace, because you are so familiar with it, but it's a fairly safe bet that if you move quickly, eat quickly and are one of life's 'rushers' then you will also talk quickly. Use situations like reading aloud stories to children, reading reports in newspapers, reading minutes at meetings to think consciously about pausing and breathing.

2. Talk about a subject and get a friend or relative (someone fairly sensitive who is a good listener) to orchestrate your pauses for you. Where there are breaks in your speech, they call out 'Pause' and you sustain the pause for the length of time of their delivery. Ask them to call out 'pause' at unpredictable moments, varying the length of time between the pauses. They can also vary the length of their calls, so that some of the pauses are short and some long. As much as possible they should try to put the pause calls in where breaks seem to occur in your content.

3. When you deliver facts, statistics, information, pause slightly before delivery. For example, when announcing yourself: 'I'm (mini-pause) Joe Bloggs.' We tend to think that facts are boring, so we rush to get them over with. Before you say your name or telephone number, pause for a moment to ensure effective delivery.

4. An ultimate deterrent for intrusive speech mannerisms. If you use ums, ers, and other hesitations then get that sensitive friend or relative to indicate to you every time you are doing them, either by a physical signal that you can see like a raised finger, or by calling 'oops' or 'beep' or something equally irritating.

5. Use a tape recorder and listen to yourself talk on a mundane subject, like what you've done that day. Play it back and listen to the number of ums and ers. Then repeat the content, keeping it free of ums and ers.

6. Notice how other people use pauses, and how they fill them in, and how this contributes to the image they project.

TONE OF VOICE

Like ideals of beauty, good taste and culture, what you consider a pleasant voice is a subjective evaluation. There can be no standardised measure for what is good and poor tone of voice. What one person considers a rich, well-educated tone, another will consider plummy and affected. Some people like the sound of 'trained' voices; others consider them over-projected and artificial. (It does, of course, depend on the sort of training.)

Even the words used to describe voice quality – thin, shrill, sharp, rich – mean different things to different people. In this section, the word 'tone' is used in its loosest sense, meaning voice quality. 'Stress' means the amount of emphasis put on a word, and is different from 'pitch', which involves a change of notes. The section will focus on the specific aspects of your sound that make someone decide they like or dislike your tone of voice.

Rhythm and Stress

The rhythm of the way you speak will be influenced by your accent and by how you use stress, that is, where you put the emphasis. In English we tend to put the emphasis on nouns. Particular patterns of rhythm can affect the way others respond to you and therefore your total image.

- Some people have a staccato, machine-gun-type delivery where they shoot short phrases at people; they can come over as curt, aggressive and reticent.

- SELF-IMPORTANT INDIVIDUALS often OVER-STRESS EVERY-THING that they SAY. Try that line stressing all the words in capitals. It makes everything sound TERRIBLY SIGNIFICANT, also pedantic and didactic. (Several politicians and public figures demonstrate this tendency, as you might expect.)

Exercises

1. To make your speech flow more smoothly and easily, use your body to help you. Your arm is going to conduct you in a different rhythm. Slowly, gently and smoothly use your hand as a baton to establish a side-to-side movement. Keep the arm and hand fairly relaxed and keep it fairly near to the body so that you don't get too tired. Move it in a straight line to and fro in front of the body in an easy, fluid motion. Then begin to talk sustaining the style of movement with the arm. It is impossible to use a staccato delivery in speech while the arm is moving in this easy, gentle way. This exercise is easier if you have someone to monitor your arm and to check when you start to speak that it does not change pace. Some people do this exercise under the table at meetings, and you can certainly do it on the phone, provided you have some privacy.

2. When you overstress, people will soon stop listening to you. Play around with a sentence, putting the stress in different places, and seeing how little you can use to make sense of what you are saying. A tape recorder can help.

Pitch and Resonance

Many of us like low-pitched voices because we associate high notes with tension. Some people habitually pitch lower than is natural for them, in the hope that their voices will sound cool and authoritative. If you do this, you may find that you get hoarse, or that you have problems being heard in situations where there is a lot of background noise, like parties.

It is the high notes that help our sound carry. High notes are not unattractive, and a naturally light voice, using plenty of pitch including high notes, can be very pleasant. When we are struck with panic or tension, the throat muscles tense and this can cause pitch to rise in an uncontrolled fashion, creating a shrill tone. This problem is more prevalent in women because they have shorter vocal chords than men and therefore a higher range of pitch. This can lead to misinterpretation. A woman can make a rational statement, but because she is apprehensive about speaking her pitch can soar, leading her to sound emotionally out of control.

The way you use pitch can be determined by the sort of accent you have or were brought up with. Some accents, like Welsh, use a wide range of pitch, while Standard English uses a narrower band. Pitch can be notated like music, and predominant patterns will influence the impression you make when you speak. If you take a question: 'Will you do me a favour?' and ask it with an upward inflection at the end, you will convey a different intention from asking the same question with a downward inflection. The first time the question seems open to any sort of reply, the second seems to be posed with the assumption that you will get the favour done. If you use upward inflection a great deal, then you will seem as though you are seeking confirmation, and possibly approval. There will not be a great deal of resolution in the tone of your voice.

On the other hand, if you use a lot of falling inflection at the end of phrases and sentences, everything will sound very definite, cut and dried, with perhaps little scope for negotiation. This pattern could antagonise or alienate people in certain situations. In my opinion, the use of pitch and inflection can exert a considerable influence over how we are regarded by others, without either knowing why. Here are two case histories:

A nne, a psychologist, said that she had problems with patients and felt that she was not gaining their trust or getting them to 'open up' to her. Her appearance was attractive and she had a pleasant manner, but when she spoke she used dropping inflections a great deal. The tone of her voice was not inviting and although the words she used were encouraging the way she spoke was not. She soon learned to ask questions with upward inflection at the end, that expressed her genuine interest and concern for her patients.

Andrew was a warm, charming man, but he seemed to be very poor at interview technique. It was also difficult to have a flowing conversation with him, though he seemed interested in the other person and had plenty to say for himself. It soon became clear that when he spoke, he tailed off and up at the end of sentences, losing energy and gaining pitch. There was no sense whatsoever that he had finished what he was saying, so the other person never knew whether it was their turn to speak. The interchange was inevitably stilted, with a lot of interruptions, and to an extent the other person felt rather ill-at-ease. After a few weeks of exercises, Andrew abandoned the habit.

Pitch Exercises

Do these exercises if you:

- have problems controlling pitch.

- confuse pitch and volume.

- would like to extend the pitch range you use when you speak.

- use a dominant and limiting pitch pattern.

1. You are less likely to find your pitch going out of control if you keep the throat relaxed. Gently nod the head, to relax the front of the throat, and speak at the same time. (This is an exercise to do in the privacy of your own home and to recollect when you are at work or in a situation where your pitch is likely to shoot up.)

   Relax and open the throat by yawning and sighing. Hum and be aware how the sound is made at the lips. Practice talking y-a-w-n-i-n-g thr-o-u-g-h th-e v-o-w-e-l s-o-u-nds, k-e-e-p-i-ng th-e thr-o-a-t w-e-ll o-p-e-n. It will feel strange, but it demonstrates how through exaggeration the throat can be kept open and relaxed.

2. To separate pitch and volume: count from 1 to 10 rising in pitch, and then in volume. Check that the two qualities of the voice have remained separate. Then count 1 to 10 rising in pitch and dropping in volume simultaneously and vice versa. You can do as many permutations of these as you like; they will effectively tune up your ear and help you distinguish between pitch and volume.

3. Singing is very good for opening up the pitch range, and can help you appreciate musicality in the voice.

4. Try reading aloud, using a gesture like a raised arm whenever you start a new paragraph to help you consciously change pitch. When speaking, change pitch when you start to make a new point. Play around and discover the full extent of your pitch range.

5. A tape recorder can help you to identify a limiting pitch pattern. Again using your arm as a baton, pull your arm down to resolve a statement, where you would instinctively want to rise. Do the reverse if you overdo the downward inflections. Say the same sentence in different ways and play around with inflection, pushing the pitch up on different words.

Note: High-frequency notes can be exaggerated by poor quality recording equipment.

Resonance

Your tone of voice is affected by your resonance balance, that is, the space available in the body for sound waves to travel through, particularly in the chest, throat, nose, face and mouth. The size of these cavities, and the extent to which they are used will affect your sound quality, in the same way that a cello and violin produce different tones, because of the difference in size. A shift in the resonance balance can create the appearance of a pitch change.

Margaret Thatcher, for example, speaks with a lot of resonance at the back of the throat, giving her plummy tones and creating the impression that her voice is lower than it is. To change a voice to the extent she has takes a lot of training.

Often, voice quality changes when you have a cold. As your nose is blocked, sound cannot be released through it. Many of us who live in cities, and areas where there is a lot of pollution, have the reverse problem in that we release too much sound through the nose, giving our voices a strident, nasal quality. There is an easy test of whether you are using too much nasality. Take a word with some nasal sounds and a vowel, like 'moon' or 'man', say it normally, then pinch your nose as you say it. If there is a noticeable change in the vowel sound when the nose is pinched, then you have obviously been releasing that sound through the nose rather than the mouth. Take the words slowly, so that you consciously make the 'm' and 'n' in the nose and make the vowel sounds in the mouth. Exercising the soft palate, at the top and back of the mouth, can help, as a lazy soft palate can make the tone nasal. Repeat 'ng, car, gar', firmly, being aware that the placement of the sounds is shifting from the nose on 'ng' to the mouth for 'car, gar'. You should be able to sense the soft palate working to shift the sounds.

You can sense resonance working by making sound and beating your chest Tarzan-style, or by placing your hands on the sides of your face around the sinuses and feeling the vibrations. Opera singers develop their resonators so that they work extremely effectively and give their voices 'carrying' power. Most of us do not need to do this, but if you want to do a 'cosmetic surgery' job on the tone of your voice you should seek the help of a voice teacher.

CLEAR SPEECH

During the agonies of puberty, many youngsters start to mumble. Teenage boys, in particular, become hyper-sensitive about their voices; understandably, as the voice when it is breaking becomes an unreliable and unpredictable instrument. When we feel self-conscious and confused about our identity we may become reluctant to let our voices out. Remember, your voice is an announcement to the world of your identity.

If you mumble, you will convey reticence and a lack of commitment when you speak. You will have difficulty encouraging others to feel confident in your presence, because you are 'contained'. Your behaviour will influence theirs. This containment can come over as distantness, and someone who is seeking involvement with you could find your 'distance' powerful and threatening. In this situation again, the differing needs we have for involvement and detachment, and the way we express these, can cause conflict.

Facial muscles stiffen up very easily, and with little use they can easily set in a mask. You are then effectively depriving yourself of one of your best visual aids, an animated face. When animals are threatened, they pull their mouths back at the sides, revealing their teeth in potential retaliation. To an extent we do the same thing, as part of our 'flight or fight' response (see Chapter Four). Our masks 'set' with tension in our faces pulling back and sideways. In some individuals, this instinct manifests itself as a nervous smile, others develop a nervous mannerism of stretching the mouth to the sides when they speak. Rigidity in the face will affect how others perceive you, and therefore your image. The impression you create is made by combinations of behavioural quirks. For instance, if your face is immobile and you use too much downward inflection, then you could seem remote and inaccessible, possibly stand-offish. With poor eye contact and little movement in the face, you might seem evasive or frightened.

The body forms the voice into speech through the speech organs, the jaw, the tongue, the mouth, the teeth and the lips. These parts give the voice shape and energy to make it into speech. For speech to be clear and projected, the muscles in these organs need to be active and free of tension. When these organs are constricted in any way, you are not letting your voice out.

The jaw is a very common site of tension in the body and we have an understandable resistance to relaxing it. We associate the need to release the jaw with the dentist's chair. When someone gets angry you can usually spot the jaw tensing up. Grinding your teeth is an indication that you hold a lot of tension in the jaw. Sometimes if you have had ill-fitting crown and bridge work done, you can instinctively try to adjust your 'bite' through teeth grinding. Nowadays, dentists realise that jaw tension can be quite a problem for their patients and they have techniques to alleviate it.

Tension in the jaw can often lend people a disapproving air, and make the speech sound as though it is being delivered through clenched teeth. As tension travels quickly, a tense jaw is often accompanied by a stiff upper lip, literally. We associate this with bravery, and certainly it indicates suppression of emotion. In fear, the upper lip trembles. A typical upper-class English accent is characterised by the stiff upper lip.

Your 'speaking image' can benefit greatly from precision and clarity. The consonants represent the quality of logic and structured thinking in speech. When we get drunk the logic blurs and so do the consonants, producing typically 'thick' speech. Lazy, sloppy speech indicates lack of commitment and energy, even arrogance: you don't care and you can't be bothered. You can improve lazy speech by doing lots of tongue-twisters, regularly. Too much tension, on the other hand, will make you seem over-contained and ill-at-ease with yourself. The happy medium is when the muscles in the face are relaxed, not flaccid, but limbered.

Left: A rigid, tense face which will not encourage others to communicate.

Right: Expressive and looking more relaxed and accessible.

Exercises for Clarity of Speech

Do these exercises if:

- you want to polish up your speech generally.

- you are always being asked to repeat yourself.

- you suspect you look and sound boring when you talk.

- you stumble over words when you get tired.

- your face twitches when you get nervous.

Almost everyone can benefit from articulation exercises: they keep the speech in top condition. Conventional elocution exercises, the 'Peter Piper picked a peck of pickled pepper' sort, can work well, but they must be done with lots of energy and precision. Before you do anything, though, you should release the jaw. Stroke it open gently, bearing in mind that the bottom jaw drops down and back when it opens. Some of us develop the habit of thrusting the bottom jaw forward whenever we speak (suggesting

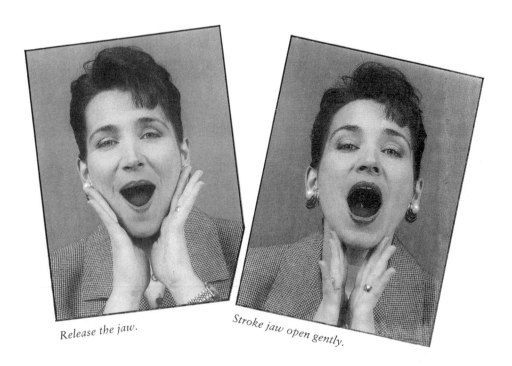

Release the jaw.

Stroke jaw open gently.

an aggressive manner). Yawning can help release the jaw, as can the following exercise from the Alexander Technique.

1. Breathe in, let the eyes light up, the cheeks smile, release the jaw open, with the tongue resting behind the bottom teeth and exhale on an easy 'a-a-a-h-h-h'. Do this several times, until you start to feel relaxed and then speak a sentence at the end of a slightly shorter 'a-a-h-h-'. This exercise will help you associate speech with exhalation and a relaxed jaw.

2. Massage the face, particularly the temples and around the lips to warm up the muscles. Scrunch the face up and stretch it lengthways, widthways and forwards. Stretch the lips back and forward (like an inverted megaphone) by repeating 'way-way-way'. Focus on the forward stretch.

a-a-a-h-h-h

Stretch lips back and forward by repeating 'way'.

3. Blow out the lips with a 'brrrr', like horses do. This is an interesting action that we often perform instinctively after rising to a challenge. We release breath out when we do it, and we relax those lips that have been tightly held together in determination. It is also the 'acid test' of the stiff upper lip. If you can't do it, then you've got one.

4. A quick way to get all the muscles going is to imagine that you are talking to someone who is entirely lip-reading all that you are saying. Do not use any more voice, just a lot more energy in the articulation, and focus on opening your mouth a lot more. When poker-faced individuals do this, they often become a lot more animated. They feel as though they are exaggerating wildly, but to the rest of us they just look as though they are communicating with more enthusiasm. This is a useful pre-speaking warm-up. (See photographs on page 122.) If you suspect you need to work more in the front of the face all the time, then it is worth getting constructive feedback from someone. You don't want to end up over-articulating, which produces a highly patronising impression. We see this in some people who've had too many elocution lessons, and in others when they speak to anyone who doesn't have an English accent.

PROJECTING THE VOICE

To project your image effectively, you also need to project your voice well. If you always speak quietly, people will assume that you are timid. They will also get tired and irritated at having to listen so attentively to you.

If your breathing and articulation are working well, then you should not have any problem with projection. Sometimes there can be a psychological 'block' on projecting the voice; the person concerned is so cripplingly shy or withdrawn that they just do not want the sound to reach others. In such a case, psychological help is needed.

The 'stage whisper' is an intense sound that travels to the back of the stalls, without the actor using any voice from the throat. The vocal chords in the larynx do not come together to create a whisper, in the way that they come together to meet the breath for voiced sound. So the power of the whisper depends on the breath and articulation control of the actor. It is energy in articulation that projects the voice.

Whispering is a useful exercise for those of you who try to project your voices by snapping together the vocal chords and straining in the throat.

121

No expression.

Animated speech.

Enthusiastic articulation.

You can also get yourself used to throwing sound by taking sounds like 'ho', 'hah' and 'hee', fixing your eye on spots at various distances, and throwing the sound to them (the vocal chords remain open to make the 'h' sound). Sometimes a physical movement like a bowling or throwing motion as you make the sound can help the sensation of it travelling. The breathing and articulation exercises given earlier can help. Remember especially 'I pause and I breathe', number 3 in the breathing section, and exercise 4 in the clarity section, where articulation was exaggerated as though the speaker was being lip-read.

Practise a 'ho' sound.

Practise saying 'hah'.

Practise saying 'hee'.

Have you ever been in the unfortunate position of sitting in a restaurant next to the bore with the intrusively loud voice? Too much volume, or volume that is sustained at the same level can make you seem overbearing and insensitive to others. Occasionally people over-project because of deafness.

If your voice is naturally clear and loud, you can use a drop in volume to effect. When you have a really important point to make, or you are talking about a subject on which you have very strong feelings, a temporary, controlled drop in volume that will make your listeners work a little harder for a short while, is a good attention-holding device.

CARE OF THE VOICE

Here are some tips:

- To stop your voice getting tired, focus on your breathing and articulation, the aspects that provide energy for the speech.

- If you have any sort of persistent hoarseness, croakiness, pain when speaking or you lose your voice often, then have a medical check-up before having speech or voice therapy.

- Professional singers often avoid dairy products before a big concert, because these stimulate the production of mucus which can coat the vocal chords and make the tone less clear.

- Your voice is like any other organ and muscle in your body, it needs to be treated with respect and it deserves rest. If a professional actor is doing a particularly demanding piece, he or she will warm up the voice beforehand and 'cool it down', as it were, afterwards by doing some gentle voice exercises. Warm up that voice before you make a presentation, ask for a pay rise, chair a meeting, and it won't let you down.

- Voices are affected by an excess of alcohol; smoking is a major contributory cause to cancer of the larynx.

- If you eat large meals late at night, regurgitated acid from the stomach can settle on the vocal chords, and cause gruffness in the morning.

- Dry air, central heating and air conditioning are bad for the voice. If necessary, you might want to buy a humidifier. Your voice is under most stress in dry smoky atmospheres with a lot of background noise, in planes and pubs and at parties, for example.

WHAT ABOUT ACCENT

There is no doubt that your accent is significant in terms of your total image. Many of us hold prejudices towards certain accents because of political associations (like South African); because of the sound quality of an accent (the Birmingham accent, for instance, is pitched in a minor key, which gives it a melancholy timbre); because of snobbery (the Cockney accent being associated with lack of class or education); or because of inverted snobbery (from those with regional accents towards those with upper-class English voices). Very few of us admit to these prejudices, because we know that they are irrational and bigoted; nevertheless, they persist. We make a strong association between certain accents and personal qualities; advertisers like to use a Yorkshire accent to sell bread and beer, for example, because that particular accent has connotations of honesty, directness, down-to-earth goodness, old-fashioned values.

In Britain, the 'preferred' accents are those of 'Standard English' – BBC English or 'Received Pronunciation' (RP) – and educated versions of other accents. Broadly speaking, RP is what is spoken by the majority of middle-class people in the South of England. As society changes, so does RP. In Noël Coward's heyday, speakers of RP rolled their 'r' sounds so that they sounded ter-r-r-ribly ter-r-r-ibly precise when they spoke. Nowadays, that has stopped and RP shows a far stronger London influence, the effect of increased informality among people in the public eye.

We also hear what has been called 'marked RP', an exaggerated version of this, with 'orf' for 'off' and so on. This is typically upper-class speech and it is dying out. There is quite a lot of prejudice towards this form of the accent, because of the associations of privilege, conservatism and class-consciousness connected with it. Generally, the least 'preferred' accents are those that are obviously working class – Birmingham, Glasgow, Liverpool, Belfast. We are still, it seems, a nation of snobs.

Some of this prejudice relates to why people adapt and modify their accent. We may do so to make ourselves understood, and so that we can fit in and be accepted. An accent can get in the way of your message. It is likely that if you went through the 'melting pot' experience of further education and you are keen to adapt to others, then you will have adapted a strong regional accent. Of course, some people cling on to and even accentuate their native accents to make a statement. There is a particular feminist writer and broadcaster who uses an extremely strong version of her accent to assert her uncompromising attitudes and working-class roots. She obviously wants to be heard as a 'woman of the people'. This accent varies in strength according to her co-debaters – usually the 'posher' the opposition, the stronger it becomes. We all have a 'wedge' of accent that we use: the more confident you are and the better your ear, the wider the range of accent you will have at your disposal. Most of us recognise the voice and accent that is obviously put on just for the phone, even if we don't use one ourselves.

So accents have certain associations, but some of the impression they make on us is due to the balance of sound in an accent. The vowel sounds of words carry the emotional content, while the consonants convey the energy and logic. An accent like Southern Irish, with imprecise consonants and lengthened vowels, will have a softness and musicality (also due to the amount of pitch range used); Glasgow, with very plosive (exploded) consonants, will seem very definite and committed and to some ears, aggressive; Standard English, with its clipped, precise consonants and falling inflection pattern, sounds confident and resolved.

Should people change their accents? There is a definite distinction to be made between good voice and speech and the 'right' accent. If you are using your natural voice well, then you should produce good, effective sound and speech whatever your accent. Sometimes people try to change their accents and this induces tension, so they start to use their voices badly to the detriment of their image. They can pick up the worst aspects of the sound that they are aspiring to, and this will make them sound affected. Often, in these cases, when the speaker gets angry or excited, the natural accent comes zooming through.

If you have been speaking with an accent for many years, then your mouth and speech organs have been used to going into certain positions to create the appropriate spaces. It can take a great deal of motivation, hard work and time to re-educate these habits. In a way, when you attempt to change your accent dramatically, you are wiping out some of your cultural heritage – almost changing your own history, if you like. Some people have the same mistaken attitude towards changing an accent as they would to having cosmetic surgery. They think that they will be newly recreated and their previous life erased. These expectations are never realised.

If you have an accent that is intrusive and so strong that it prevents you being understood by others, then you may want to 'clean up' some sounds. In which case, you need to sort out which sounds are the most impenetrable to the people around you, and work on them. You may want to seek professional help with this. As you are re-educating the habits of a lifetime it can take a lot of time and motivation.

The world would be a very boring place if we all spoke in the same way. An accent can add colour, vigour and distinctiveness to a well-produced voice and emphasise your individuality.

chapter seven

SPEAKING IN PUBLIC

T he ability to speak in public shows great confidence in your total image; and it enhances it. If you want to make youself prominent in a particular field, get yourself noticed in a company, promote yourself or your business, then you can do it cheaply and effectively by becoming a good public speaker and thrusting yourself into the limelight.

You could be one of those lucky people who seem to be naturally good at public speaking. It is unlikely that you were born with this ability. Great speakers are instinctive and inspired; they also prepare well, learn performance technique and draw heavily on experience to develop their skills. What passes for a natural ease and rapport with an audience is often a result of technique, the speaker using learned skills so well that we can't see the 'seams'.

You can learn to speak effectively in public by going on courses and reading manuals, but there is no substitute for getting out and doing it. If you dislike speaking in public, then take every opportunity to do so; even if you only start off by asking questions at the PTA meeting. Most of the advice in this chapter applies to speaking in public in all sorts of situations, be it speaking to four or five others at a meeting, or addressing an audience of three hundred at a convention.

When you speak in public, almost all the aspects that make up your total image come under scrutiny. Your posture, body language, facial expression, use of voice and appearance all matter. The focus of attention is such that it can feel as though your presentation skills are under examination through a microscope. The situation is often stressful, because the speaker is being observed and judged by others. Small quirks, like speaking too quietly or wriggling, which are not particularly noticeable in everyday communication, become intrusive and exaggerated in front of an audience.

It is hardly surprising, then, that some of us feel it is easier to pretend to be somebody else when we are speaking in public. We assume a 'public speaking image' that has nothing to do with our real selves. We sense that speaking in public is connected to acting, and so we portray stereotypical roles: 'the infallible authority', 'the super-smooth sales person', 'the successful superwoman'. Unfortunately, if we don't really feel like these types, then we will look as though we are striving for effect. For instance, you could decide that you want to play 'the life and soul of the party' when you speak, although, in actuality you are a rather quiet person who rarely uses humour. You read that humour works well in public speaking so you decide to tell a few jokes. You look ill-at-ease when you do so, and your timing leaves a lot to be desired. Your talk misfires badly. You will not have been true to yourself and your audience will have been reluctant to trust you. You need to find your own style.

The most skilled actors use their own feelings and experiences to help them inhabit character. As a public speaker you have more scope than most actors – you have your own script, direction and interpretation to follow. Why, you can even choose the costume and rearrange the set if you like. The most successful speakers are obviously projecting an image, but one that rings true. They project the best aspects of themselves, 'edited highlights'. The serious, quiet person will project serenity and consideration for others; the outrageous extrovert will use humour and shock tactics. Speaking in public is a performance, and one in which you present a heightened version of your personality.

To speak well, there needs to be a balance of impact between speaker, message and audience. If one of these elements overpowers the other two – if the speaker is over-concerned to project personality, say, or the message is rammed home without due regard for the type of audience, or the speaker allows himself or herself to be thrown by a noisy crowd – then the performance will suffer. Your total image helps maintain this balance: if you get up to speak dressed like a Christmas tree, then your appearance will be overpowering. Delivering your message in an over-stressed and therefore over-significant tone of voice will encourage your audience to switch off. When you start to speak, if your body language and facial expression remind the audience of a frightened rabbit, then you won't gain their confidence.

Both in planning and in presentation, the speaker's main consideration should be the audience. When we are in an audience, we make two important decisions about speakers. Do they have credibility (do we trust them? have they authority? do we respect them?) and can we identify with them (do they understand our problems? have we shared experiences in common? do we have any similar values?). Presenting an effective image is all about getting this balance right. Individuals in an audience will differ from one another in the extent to which they need to feel that you are someone they can look up to, or someone they can empathise with, or a mixture of these qualities. The situation matters, too. If you are delivering a lecture, then the overriding need could be that you convey credibility. As an after-dinner speaker, an understanding of the culture, mood and humour of the audience could be more relevant.

You convey credibility and audience identification through your image, and again you need to consider the audience:

Jane is a successful wife, mother and businesswoman who has been asked to address a local housewives' association. She dresses 'down', hoping to fit in better. Unfortunately, this makes the audience mistrust her credibility: some of them suspect, because she looks ill-at-ease in her casual, drab clothes and her grooming suggests someone who usually favours a tailored look, that Jane could be patronising them. Her visual image does not inspire them. She decides to impress them by recalling her professional and academic achievements (which works well when she addresses groups of her male peers in business). The housewives remain singularly unimpressed.

The next time Jane goes to speak to a similar group, she wears a smartish suit that she wears for work. She talks about her experiences and achievements as a wife and mother, alongside her professional success. The talk goes extremely well and the audience is receptive and appreciative.

The biggest block to effective public speaking is attitude. If you think you can't and you never will be able to, you won't. Speaking in public is something anyone can *learn* to do. Be positive, and accept setbacks as part of the learning process. A much-quoted statistic from the *Book of Lists* shows that 41% of Americans fear public speaking more than death!

CONQUERING NERVES

Nervousness causes an increase in the amount of adrenalin in the body. In controlled doses, adrenalin can add excitement and energy to your performance. Virtually every professional performer experiences a surge of adrenalin on the first night of a show, and the stimulus can make an excellent performance become brilliant. Often very seasoned actors and speakers are struck by nerves unexpectedly and for no apparent reason. To do their jobs well, they need to be able to keep their nervousness under control and to use it positively. You could have done a great deal to build your 'public speaking image'; it will all be wasted if on the big day your confidence and control are undermined by nerves.

Ask yourself what is the worst thing that can happen. The chances are it is not anything life-threatening. You may dry up, be asked awkward questions, stumble over some words. After your talk, life will go on. This is of course a rationalisation and may not help. It is often helpful, though, to plan something enjoyable to do after your talk; it will give you something to look forward to and prevent you brooding and analysing your performance too much.

Presumably, if someone has asked you to speak you are considered entertaining or authoritative enough for an audience to want to listen. At least, the person who has asked you to speak thinks so even if you don't. If your speaking in public is linked to work, then it is unlikely you would have been given that responsibility unless your bosses thought that you could do it. If someone at work suggests that you develop your public speaking skills, then take it as a compliment; it could well mean that they think you are destined for greater things.

It's worth taking a look at the attitudes that produce uncontrollable nerves. When you get up to speak, do you assume that you have the full attention of your audience? Do you feel undermined because the audience are focusing all their attention on you ready to scrutinise and assess you?

If you've answered 'yes' to both questions, then in my opinion you have an over-generous view of others. Ideally, of course, audiences should be immediately receptive when you start to speak. In reality, human beings being as self-absorbed as we are, many of the audience's brains will be full of mundane thoughts. They'll be wondering whether they should take the car in for a service soon, what they are going to have for lunch, whether someone is going to let some air into the room. But we don't like to seem rude and we know that we should appear attentive, so many of the audience will be feigning attention.

In reality, it is your job as speaker to get the audience's attention. You need to focus their concentration on what you are going to say. You may need to call them to attention, to tell them who you are, to establish your credentials, and to introduce your subject. When you are first before an audience, they need to adjust to how you look, sound and what you are saying. You are negotiating for their interest and attention.

Experience speakers never make the most important points during these early stages, because they know that it is a period of adjustment for the audience. Sometimes they may make controversial statements, to arouse interest, but they will never make main points in isolation without considerable expansion and repetition later on in the talk.

Some speakers regard the audience as a great big beast, out to get them. Unless you are going into a situation that you know to be hostile, this is not generally the case. I suppose if you have a pessimistic view of humanity then you could justify thinking that an audience wants you to fail. However, even people who are actively opposed to your views do not want to sit through a talk that is poorly delivered and boring. They would far rather rise to meet a greater challenge. Most audience members will want your performance to succeed, even if they want your content to fail.

If we are to believe the *Book of Lists*, there will be many people in the audience who share your nervous reaction to speaking in public, in which case the last thing they want is to see you failing. It will remind them of their own vulnerability. (There's a similar type of reaction when someone we know dies, though on a different scale. We feel grief at the loss of the person, and the loss for their family and friends, but we are also reminded of our own mortality, which for many of us is a chastening thought.)

Audiences have expectations of their relationship with a speaker. They can often feel relaxed and secure because they know that they are the observers rather than the observed ones. There is also safety in numbers. The speaker will be under greater stress and he or she will have an increased pulse rate. When an audience member asks a question, that person's pulse rate soars because he or she is suddenly being scrutinised. Indeed, the pulse rate of the audience member sitting *next* to the questioner also soars. Contrary to how we appear on the surface, it seems a great many of us shrink from public attention.

This safety in numbers leads audience members to behave in a certain way. Individuals who in a one-to-one conversation would actively encourage the speaker to continue talking by nodding the head, facial reaction and responsive murmurs do not make these signs to the same extent when they are in a group. So the speaker, who is presenting a 'heightened image' of themselves and behaving accordingly, looks to the audience for reciprocal behaviour and gets very little obvious encouragement back. To the inexperienced speaker this can be very disconcerting. But it does not mean that an audience is not appreciating what you are saying; only that people in audiences behave differently from the way they behave as individuals. Understanding this difference can be very helpful.

Following the idea that 'behaviour breeds behaviour' there is a way that you, as speaker, can influence the way your audience behaves. The more confident and relaxed you are, the more reassured they will feel about what is in store. When you speak in public, for the duration of that talk, you are effectively cast in the role of leader.

When you think about the worst thing that could happen to you, try and see it from a humorous angle. Then envisage everything going very smoothly, approbation and approval all round. Take yourself through your talk, step by step, from entering the room, feeling nervous but controlled, to leaving the building afterwards feeling pleased with yourself.

We have control over our conscious thoughts and you can choose to re-run one scenario rather than the other. If you keep dwelling on disaster, as a possibility or a memory, then you are choosing to sabotage your potential for success. Your pessimistic view of the speech may well become a self-fulfilling prophecy. Your negativity will spread. You'll probably put off preparing the talk, and you will develop a defensive attitude towards the audience which they will sense. Keep visualising your talk as a positive experience and it will become one. Genuine enthusiasm and a strong desire to reach others can more than compensate for lack of technical expertise.

You can make contingency plans for disaster, which can reduce your apprehension. Prepare a 'safety line' like: 'Excuse me, I'd just like to check in my notes to see that I've covered everything so far.' Translated it could mean: 'Where on earth am I and what comes next?' The audience, though, will be reassured that you have developed and are following a structure, and they can use the break as a rest for themselves. Sometimes, with a small audience which you can call to order easily, a break for questions can serve the same function. Be sure that you are able to keep it short, and that you can easily get back on track.

Many people who have to speak in public are also involved in the organisation of the event at which they are speaking. If this is the case, it is vital that you have some time to yourself beforehand to prepare or your speech and consequently the event as a whole will suffer. It may even be necessary to be prima donna about it. In this time, I would suggest you prepare youself physically for the task ahead. If you have sufficient time and you regularly run, swim or attend aerobics classes then use your usual form of exercise to warm up. When your body and voice are warmed up, they are far more receptive to the directions your mind transmits. Take five minutes to relax your body and try to empty your mind, so that a part of you is observng your mind which is free of any thoughts. If thoughts intrude, let them come and go. This is a meditation technique which can be immensely calming and can recharge you.

Everyone should do a mini-workout for voice and body before speaking, even if your only opportunity is a snatched five minutes in the toilet.

Remember to pay particular attention to those parts of your body that take the tension. If your knees wobble when you stand in front of an audience, you will need to shake out and warm up the legs before you start. If your face muscles twitch, then give them particular attention by massage and stretching. Detailed exercises for different parts of the body have been described in Chapters Four and Six. Here is the minimum you should do:

- Check neck and shoulders for tension by nodding head gently and rolling shoulders.

- Shake arms and legs to free tension.

- Check that breathing is low, stomach out on breath IN and in on breath OUT. Consciously blow out in a steady stream on several OUTbreaths.

- Warm up the face, gently stroke open the jaw, stretch the lips forward and backward. Blow the lips out and do a bit of 'pah, pah, pah, bah, bah, bah, mah, mah, mah', then blow the lips out. Sigh and yawn out.

- Stand tall, feeling the back of the neck lengthening and widening, and smile. If you look glad to be there, you may actually get to feel that way.

If you are struck with panic upon entering the room in which you are to speak, then run an internal monologue on what you are doing rather than thinking about the effect you are creating. For instance, 'I'm walking up to the platform, I'm breathing out, I'm looking at people and smiling at them, I'm breathing out, I'm sitting on the stage, I'm breathing out.' You should have a good sitting and standing position, in which you feel comfortable and in which you feel that you are sending out the right signals. Waiting to speak can be very daunting and nerve-racking; this is the time in which to use this position and to focus on controlling your rate of breathing by breathing out slowly. You can then be secure that you are looking good and composed, however much you are churning inside.

Remember to focus out on the audience, make contact with them. It has been suggested that if you feel intimidated by your audience then imagining them sitting there stark naked will help relax you. In some instances this could cause helpless giggles, but you might want to try it.

If you are waiting to speak, the more you can gauge the audience the better your rapport with them will be. Look out for age, social class, proportions of each sex and, with experience, you will be able to use this time to alter the angle of your speech accordingly. Decide what you are going to *do*, when you first speak, rather than trying to *be* something (funny, shocking, impressive). When we rush to create an effect, we rarely attend to the means and our intentions misfire. On the other hand, if the means are appropriate the effects often look after themselves. So you might want to welcome your audience, intrigue them, reassure them, challenge them. Just make sure that you know what you are doing, and get on and do it, rather than regarding yourself as a passive victim. Tell yourself: 'I'm introducing, I'm pausing and breathing. I'm confiding, I'm breathing. I'm describing, I'm breathing.'

All the exercises to deal with stress response as described in previous chapters can help deal with nerves. You can produce saliva in a dry mouth by gently biting the tongue or imagining yourself sucking a lemon. If you are over-producing saliva then opening the mouth a couple of times to breathe in can help dry up the excess. Sipping from a glass of water, and letting the audience know that you are going to do so, can provide another 'safety line' and break for you to gather your thoughts.

PREPARATION

Some people regard themselves as failures at public speaking because they had a bitter experience once when they were not adequately prepared to speak. They had put off thinking about the content because they were dreading the event. When the event arrived, it was every bit as bad as they expected and aggravated because of their lack of preparation.

Considering the Audience

Your main concern when starting to plan a talk should be your audience. Find out as much about them as you can beforehand. Ask yourself:

- who are the audience (age, sex, race, class, education)?

- why are they assembled?

- how much do they know about the subject?

- what is their attitude towards it?

- what instincts am I going to appeal to? (What are you offering the audience in terms of benefits for themselves? Are you offering a new concept for them to explore? Can they gain financially? Will they feel psychologically better about themselves? Does what you are saying appeal to social aspirations?)

- to what extent am I appealing to their emotions or their logic?
- what do I want them to gain from my talk?
- do I want them to do anything as a result?
- will they understand any jargon I use, or will I need to explain it?
- what are my credentials for talking to this particular audience?
- what do we have in common?
- what questions will they ask me?

When you have answered all these questions, your brain should be buzzing with ideas.

Objectives and Intentions

Your talk should have an overall objective that you can express succinctly. Within that overall objective you have various means of expressing your aims. For instance, if your purpose is to sell somebody something (and we all sell something, even if only our own credibility) then you could reassure them that you are genuine, flatter them into associating themselves with the select few who have this item or service, advise them of its advantages, insult the competition, confide in them about your own experience with the item or service and persuade them that life without it is inconceivable. You could have got them excited by challenging, insulting or humouring them. You will notice that everything the speaker does, is described as an active verb, and these are your means of achieving your objective. So you need to ask yourself: what are these *actions* that you will use as the means of getting your message over?

Sometimes the action or intention is not realised. For instance, if you wish to inform an audience and you underestimate their level of under-standing, you could end up patronising them (this often happens with over-use of visual aids). The actions you decide to take will also colour the way you deliver your content, which is as significant as the actual words used. If you decide to inspire your audience with a particular point, then your delivery will be very different from challenging them with the same point. I suggest to clients that they jot these actions down on their note cards ('inspire', 'challenge', 'involve', etc.) to keep them on track with their objective and help them change the voice for different points. Using this method, you never need think 'I don't know what I'm doing' because you have prepared your actions.

Selecting and Organising your Material

So far you have considered your audience, your objective and what are the actions (intentions) of your talk. You now need to gather and organise your material. The ideas of your talk matter far more than the actual words. If you have considered and investigated your ideas and feel enthusiasm for them, then you are off to a flying start. I am not going to dwell too long on organisation of material, because there are plenty of good books on the subject (see Directory). Don't fix your content too early because ideas will come to you over a period of time.

One of the most effective methods of organising material is to put your main objective in the centre of a sheet of paper and then to place other related points randomly around it. Keep adding to the surrounding points until you can think of no more, then start to put them into a logical sequence, discarding those that are irrelevant. A version of this method that employs 'right-brain thinking' (mentioned in the eye contact section of Chapter Four) suggests that to free the imagination in the under-used right lobe, you draw your objective and all the relevant points in terms of pictures. This method does seem to stimulate imagination and the memory is more effective at recalling ideas in terms of visual images than in words.

When you speak to an audience, you take them on a clearly signposted journey, so the more logical the structure the better. It makes sense to arrange material so that it follows a cause–problem–solution and/or topical, chronological or geographical arrangement. Let me demonstrate – I am giving a talk on 'Developing an Image':

Cause/problem/solution: you haven't had time to think about your image/ You are presenting yourself badly/Come on one of my seminars and buy this book!

Chronological: how over six months you could improve your image, with a month-by-month programme.

Geographical: how Europe and America compare in this area/what we have got from America and Europe/what else is to come from those continents.

It will be clear from this example that some subjects suit certain structures far better than others and that you should pick the structure that is easiest to follow, both for your sake and the sake of your audience. The chronological and geographical structures in the above example seem contrived and obscure. The first arrangement of offering a solution to a problem is obviously effective if you are persuading someone or trying to sell them something. If you are keen to make a particularly rational appeal, then pre-empt your audience's questions. Describe a problem, suggest, consider and dismiss other solutions, and then lead your audience through an exploration of your idea. You will have demonstrated your powers of intellect and reasoning and flattered the audience by assuming that they have the intelligence to understand your case.

Don't try to cover too much material. The audience will absorb your idea if you keep the structure simple and illustrate the points you are making with anecdotes, examples and comparisons.

Devices

We assimilate information more effectively in some forms than others. Odd numbers of points, lists of three (like faith, hope and charity), parallels (something is like something else) and comparisons (on the one hand … on the other) work well. We remember odd numbers better than even numbers because they form a clearer pattern for the brain.

When you start to speak there is a period of adjustment during which the audience adapts to you. You will be speaking at a rate of roughly 130–150 words a minute, while the brains of your audience can process words at about three times that speed. Inevitably, then, the audience's attention wanders. In order to grab their attention at the beginning and to maintain interest throughout your talk you need to create 'attention-getters': controversial statements, questions (rhetorical or otherwise), impersonations, changes of position, jokes, differences in vocal levels, all help arouse and maintain interest. Audience concentration strays after about ten minutes, so if you are giving a long talk, then break it up with frequent attention-getters.

Most people realise that a punchy opening is important, but many forget that the punchy conclusion is even more so. After all, it is the last thing that your audience hears you say, so it should be the most memorable.

If a speaker feels in any way apologetic, he or she will often overrun as compensation and to try and make amends. Of course, rambling on detracts even more from a performance. If a punchy ending has been prepared, one that ends on an upnote, it can be delivered within the alloted time and conclude the case. A clean, succinct ending can do wonders for a wobbly start and flabby middle.

Be imaginative about the devices you use. The more accessible you make yourself and the more you relate to your audience the better. If you can get a response from them early on, that helps. You are acknowledging them and involving them, and they usually like it. Remember that people are less inhibited in large groups, and that a response like laughter becomes contagious quickly.

Notes

You will need to decide how you are going to deliver your talk. I am horrified at the number of presentations given by people who read every word from a script. This is not speaking, but reading aloud. The written word and the spoken word sound very different; we do not, for instance, punctuate speech in the same way as a written text. When you read a speech verbatim, you effectively create a substantial barrier between you and your audience. So, if you care about your subject and your audience, speak from notes. People often use scripts because they do not feel confident about speaking, but by doing so they never get any better. (Politicians use written speeches so that press quotes are carefully controlled.)

Your notes should effectively convey the ideas of your talk. You won't need to put down whole sentences, just words, idea headings. You could also want to note quotations, figures and statistics which can be difficult to remember and have more clout when they are read, rather than conjured up out of thin air. You can also put down intentions, if on a particular point you want to *reassure* for instance, and instructions to yourself, like *tranparency, pause, breathe* etc. Use different coloured pens and write legibly.

Most people use more notes than they need. Time and time again people talk about subjects they know a great deal about, with a wad of notes that they never look at. The notes are there as a 'baby blanket', a reassuring safety net. As you rehearse your talk you should keep refining your notes; get them down to the absolute minimum that you can manage with.

Audiences are very impressed by fluent speakers who talk without using notes. If you know your subject well, and can carry a clear structure in your head (that could just be headings for three points), then you should leap in. If this all seems a bit too drastic, you can always leave your notes on a table or lectern, rather than holding them, to provide a lifejacket should you start to drown. Never, ever, learn a speech off by heart. What the audience will see then is someone remembering words (the activity of remembering is indicated through eye movement), rather than a speaker whose prime concern is to get a message over to them.

Timing

There's an old show-business adage, 'always leave them wanting more', which is also relevant to speaking in public. Unfortunately, audiences are pre-conditioned to anticipate public speaking as a rather torturous experience. So even if you are the most riveting of speakers you will rise even further in the audience's estimation if you finish slightly before the prescribed time, rather than running over.

If you are asked to give a long speech or talk, remember that it's your show and you can choose what to do with the time. Given forty minutes, you could decide to talk for half an hour and then spend the last ten minutes receiving questions.

Rehearsing

As soon as you have a rough map of the content, start expressing your ideas aloud. Many speakers mistakenly spend hours poring over their plans and notes and never deliver the material – fatal! Expressing your ideas aloud will help you to choose what points to include and what to leave out – some will be easier to articulate than others. Get feedback when you rehearse, from colleagues, family, friends or a professional consultant. Ask them whether they think you are achieving your objective and get them to analyse content and style, critically. You may feel self-conscious doing this, but it can be a great help. Encourage them to point out any nervous mannerisms or intrusive gestures that you are making.

Tape and video recorders are useful rehearsal aids, as long as you don't start posturing and adding artificial touches to create effects. Remember that what is being recorded is a stage in the process: the polished performance can only be achieved in the presence of an audience. Keep asking yourself if you are sticking to your actions, those intentions (the verbs) that you have towards the audience. It is your interaction with them that matters.

It is better to rehearse for half an hour every day for several weeks, than to spend a whole desperate day rehearsing twenty-four hours before you are due to speak. The benefits are obviously cumulative. Don't let fear of the event put you off doing it. Practice pays and it need not be tedious. Good speakers keep thinking creatively, adding to and subtracting from their material right up until the moment they deliver it.

Visual Aids

Visual aids should enhance your talk, rather than acting as something for you to hide behind. Some speakers leap at the opportunity of using slides, because they think the darkness helps them become anonymous. Your talk should stand on its own; visual aids help convey facts, statistics and ideas that are difficult to put over in words. They also help the audience retain information because our response to visual impact is so strong.

Your visual aids should help your total image as speaker. They should look professional and be clearly visible. If you overdo them, using too many, and reading aloud a great deal of what can clearly be seen, then you risk insulting the intelligence of your audience. If you use your visual aids as an *aide mémoire* and talk to the aids rather than the audience, you will appear inconsiderate and you will lose the audience. Remember *you* are your most powerful visual aid.

If using handouts, it's a good idea to give them out at the end of your talk. That way, they don't provide a distraction for the audience while you are speaking.

ON THE DAY

Arrangement of the Room

When you get to the place where you are speaking, you need to check that the seating arrangements and facilities are as you would like them. You must be able to be seen and heard by your audience. The greater the physical barriers between you and them, the less accessible you become.

If the audience are seated behind desks or you choose to deliver your talk from behind a lectern or table then communication will not be as direct and open as it could be. Lots of speakers like speaking behind a lectern, because only the top half of the body is visible and so audience members can't see those shaking knees or twitchy feet. A lectern is a symbol of authority but, more effectively, it acts as a barrier and can dwarf small speakers. With your whole body on display the audience has more of you to scrutinise, and if you look comfortable with this exposure you gain power. You seem to have nothing to hide. If you want to use a lectern, you could use it as a base to which you return occasionally and use this repositioning to maintain interest from the audience.

Sometimes seating is fixed, and it is impossible to do anything about it. Where possible, though, you may want to rearrange any seating that is too reminiscent of the classroom, to make it more informal. People are most accessible when they are seated in a circle or a semi-circle. In this arrangement, it is easier to have more direct contact with every member of the audience; you lessen the chance of the back row dozing off.

The seating plan can have a powerful psychological effect on audience and speaker. The most daunting arrangement for the speaker is amphitheatre style, like many university lecture theatres, where the speaker is at ground level with the audience looking down from a raked semi-circle. If you are nervous, this can make you feel very small, insignificant and overwhelmed.

A speaker elevated on a stage is accorded authority through positioning. The audience is already literally looking up to you. The different levels do create distance between you and your audience, which could make it more difficult to identify with them and to make them feel relaxed.

Check that the temperature of the room is as you would like it, and that it is adequately ventilated. You can't expect to inspire an audience if they are sitting in an over-heated stuffy room after a heavy, alcoholic lunch.

Make sure that you are well lit, and that everyone can see you. If you are standing in shadow your audience will find it a strain to focus on you for long. Check all your equipment before you start, and if you are using a microphone try out the level. If you are fortunate enough to have the free run of the room before your audience arrive, then it is a good idea to have a mini-rehearsal of snatches of your talk, so that you can feel how much you need to project your voice, and how 'large' you need to be. This can also help to make you feel you've established the room as your territory.

Rapport with the Audience

You can lose track of your structure, stumble over the odd word, let your nerves show at the outset, but if you establish a good rapport with the audience you will win them over. To some extent, establishing rapport is a matter of your attitude. If you believe that you have something valid to say, and are enthusiastic about communicating it to others, then they will receive it in a positive manner. Here are some tips:

- Always stand rather than sit. Your energy level is different when you stand and you look more powerful. Sitting is a more defensive position because you are already protecting some of the body. In some situations, a policeman addressing a group of children perhaps, sitting is more appropriate: sitting brings you to the same level as the audience. Stand tall and well. If you are giving a long talk, like a lecture or training session, then at least stand at the outset to establish authority. When you sit, you become more like one of the audience, so it's a good tactic when you want them to feel relaxed and you want to gain their confidence, during the question-and-answer session perhaps.

- Establish base territory for yourself, that is, get yourself standing still and comfortable in one spot. The more space that surrounds this spot the better. We tend to cling to furniture and objects. If an empty room has just one piece of furniture in it, then when people enter, they will immediately go to that piece of furniture. It acts as a support. The more support-free you can be the better. You can leave base territory and move around, but at the outset it is worth showing the audience that you can stand comfortably in one spot.

- Avoid showing 'flight' instinct through dancing around, squirming and wiggling the hips, foot-tapping, pushing off from the heels like a ballerina about to 'jeter'. Root those feet in that hangar.

- Leave the front of the body unprotected, if you can. If you look defensive, the audience will doubt your credibility and sincerity. Standing with your hands folded in front of the body, you are in what's known as the 'fig-leaf' position. We put our hands over areas that we feel are in need of protection. This position is also reminiscent of a vicar about to launch into evensong and most feel daunted at the prospect of a sermon. Standing with your hands behind your back can look very formal and as though you are on patrol like a policeman or sergeant major. Your hands can get locked in this position so that you prevent yourself using natural gestures.

People put themselves into extraordinary positions when they speak in public. A man on one of my courses held his bottom all the way through his talk. (I expect Freud would have had something to say about that.) Try standing with your arms and hands hanging loose and free at the sides. If they feel tense, try to relax the shoulders and gently shake the arms and fingers to release them. Don't play with anything in your hands, and use gesture naturally.

- Stand still, look and smile at your audience, breathe out, before you start to speak. Nerves make many people start speaking as they move up to their spot, and before the audience knows what is happening they are off and running. Remember that the start of a talk is a period of adjustment for an audience.

- Don't clear your throat before you speak, unless you have a heavy cold and you know that your vocal cords are covered with mucus. Throat-clearing is a nervous mannerism, and an amateur one. It informs the audience that you are about to use your voice, and that you need to check that it is working. Swallow hard, or have a sip of water. Throat-clearing is also a device to get attention and you should trust your attention-getting opening to do that for you.

- Make steady eye contact with the audience. If you move your eyes too quickly you will look nervous and the audience will begin to feel the same way. With a small audience you should be able to sustain eye contact for a sufficient length of time to acknowledge each person as an individual. With a large audience, you'll need to have spots where you rest your eyes for a moment and then sweep on to the next one. These spots will need to be dotted around the auditorium so that you include everyone in your gaze. If you don't make eye contact with the back of the hall, it is unlikely that your voice will reach the back row either.

- Do not be tempted by a friendly face into thinking, 'Thank goodness, someone likes me, I'll deliver my talk to them', then proceed to make eye contact with that person to the exclusion of everyone else. The chosen individual will soon start to feel embarrassed and the rest of the audience will feel excluded. You need to make good steady eye contact with those members of the audience who are looking cynical and bored. This takes courage, but it works. Indeed, someone who appears down-right awkward and resistant in an audience can be looking like this because they feel superior to everyone else and/or because the subject is a threatening one to them. By making extra eye contact with them, they start to feel that you are acknowledging their significance, and they feel less threatened because they trust you more.

- The better your eye contact with an audience, the more responsive you are to their needs and moods. That is why, if you know your subject well, then speaking without the distraction of notes allows you the most effective interaction. Do not regard the audience as an impersonal entity. Members of it will sense that you are doing that and react against it.

143

Maintaining steady eye contact can help you to notice if audiences are looking bored or dubious, and do something to awaken their interest or to amplify your argument. If there is a lot of shuffling, coughing and movement going on, then you have probably aroused hostility or have been rambling on for too long. Sometimes when you are speaking in public it can be a shock to look at the audience and find that they are operating at a very different energy level from you. As performer and the observed one you are making extra effort to communicate; the recipients and observers can be much more relaxed. In audiences generally, there is a feeling that the role of listening is a shared one and so individuals are less responsive than they would be in one-to-one conversation. That does not mean that they are not absorbing or enjoying what you are saying. I am still constantly surprised by audience members who look bored, disapproving or cynical during a talk, and then come up at the end and say how interesting they found it.

- Use pauses to give yourself rests, and to let your audience know that you have finished a point, before you move on to the next one.

- If you are in doubt, ask people whether they can hear you. Do not throw your voice up to the ceiling to make it carry; if the room you are in has a difficult acoustic, then throw your voice to a point about two-thirds of the way along the floor and that should suffice.

- Use technique to keep interest. Lower your voice and make the tone intimate (your action being 'confiding') if you are saying something really important. Most of us love to think that we are sharing a confidence. Use pause to build up suspense. Tone of voice can be used as an attention-getter.

- If something goes wrong – you drop your notes, your slide projector breaks down, you get your words jumbled, someone in the audience has a fit – then don't pretend that it hasn't happened. Deal with it and get on with your talk. Honesty is the best policy and a quality that audiences respond to.

- Personalise your talk and reveal your own experiences and personality. You will seem authoritative if you are matter-of-fact about your achievements; your audience will identify with you if you reveal your own weaknesses and don't adopt a 'holier than thou attitude'. Get a response from your audience as much as possible – be it nods of agreement, giggles of acknowledgement, noises of disapproval at something controversial. You can comment on these responses and play off them: 'Some of you are looking a bit confused so I'll explain that again' or 'I can see some of you have had experience of this.' You are speaking for their benefit and it is their response that matters most.

Taking Questions

People ask questions for all sorts of reasons. They might want to attract attention to themselves and make some point they feel strongly about; they might want to show support for you as speaker; they could want to undermine you; or, finally, they could actually want some further information or to know your opinion about something.

Unless you want to risk constant interruption to your flow, it is wise to keep questions to a stipulated time, usually at the end of your talk. Listen to the question and repeat it for the benefit of the rest of the audience, if you suspect that the questioner was unclear. Take your time to answer it, and don't worry about being seen to think. The audience will find this more reassuring than a glib answer delivered off pat. If someone is being deliberately awkward then try and find out why, but remember that you have the floor and so if they start being a nuisance you can suggest that other people have questions and that you and the questioner can continue the dialogue privately, later on. Under pressure you can always use the deflecting techniques used by politicians, for instance: 'I'm not sure how relevant that is at this moment. What I do think is relevant, though, is ...' (Irritating, this, but effective, if TV interviews are anything to go by.)

How you answer questions is very important. The more hostile the questions, the more open and relaxed your expression, body language and voice are the better. Let people know they will be able to ask questions at the end, and that they can store them up. If nobody asks one don't look uncomfortable. You can always say, 'Something I'm often asked is ...' or ask the audience a question, 'Have any of you experience of...'

If you are asked a question which you cannot answer, don't bluff. Be honest, and suggest somewhere or somebody who might be able to supply the information. Sometimes a fellow audience member is all too happy to oblige.

WHAT TO WEAR

Through our clothes we indicate to what extent we see ourselves as decorative or functional. We indicate how much attention we want others to pay to our appearance and presentation, and how much attention we want our message to receive. High heels, tight skirts, lots of jewellery, elaborate hair and make-up are obviously not Action Woman clothes. Action men wouldn't get very far in velvet jackets, frilly shirts and tight pants.

When speaking in public it is important that your appearance does not overpower the message. Of course, show-business personalities often dress in a very flamboyant style, and their appearance becomes an expected part of their image. Were they to turn up to speak in a sober suit, they could well disappoint the expectations of the audience. For those of us who have less extrovert images, our 'costumes' can help us project our personalities and message to an audience. If you are billed as an authority on a subject, then you will help your case if you look responsible and dignified. As an after-dinner speaker you will be cast more in the role of an entertainer, and a dressier style, as befits the occasion, could work better.

As your 'public speaking image' is a heightened version of yourself, do not compromise your individuality in order to identify with your audience. If you are speaking to a group of women who are returning to work after having had children, they don't want to see someone who looks just like them, they want to see someone who behaves and thinks like them but looks like a successful business woman. You want to inspire them to think, 'yes, I could do that'. As a male entrepreneur addressing a group of small-business owners, the same thing holds true. You need to look inspiring and like an example to follow.

It is often more effective to develop the identification element through your behaviour and content than through your appearance, with just a hint of identification element in your outfit. A woman speaking to an all-male audience might want to wear a tailored jacket for example; a man addressing a women's group might wear a slightly more flamboyant tie than usual or a polo shirt. I think it is always glaringly obvious and patronising to an audience to go overboard: for instance, the woman who addresses her all-male audience in a severe pin-striped suit or the man who addresses his largely female audience wearing a loud tie and pink shirt.

The audience might not be well turned out, but they expect you to be so. Grooming is important, all of you is on show, and you insult an audience if you turn up looking unkempt. Remember that your visual image is the most potent one. It's not always a good idea to wear new clothes; you could find out that the skirt rides up or that the trousers are too tight, and you need to feel comfortable. Wear something that fits generously, so that you can throw your arms open in expansive gestures if you so wish. Large patterns and loud colours over large expanses can overpower you, and tire the eyes of your audience. Wear detail and colour near the face, to draw attention there.

RADIO AND TV APPEARANCES

An executive from an oil company was interviewed on television about an oil slick that was the responsibility of his company. His performance on television was excellent – he oozed honesty and integrity. He was there primarily to defend his company and he succeeded in doing this and far more, taking the opportunity to do some very positive public relations work. As a direct result of his appearance, investment in the oil company soared.

This story illustrates just how significant media appearances can be – for you and your own business or for the company that employs you. Viewers remember the impression they received far more than what was actually said. So it is important to appear relaxed, controlled and confident.

Although millions of people could be listening to and watching you, the more intimate your manner the more effective it will be. Talk directly to the interviewer, and don't feel that you need to say too much or have to keep talking. Pauses are the responsibility of the interviewer. Do not allow him or her to pressurise you (see breathing exercises in Chapter Six) and take time to think out the answers if you need to. You should have anticipated the questions you are likely to be asked, and prepared the content. Sometimes the interviewer will run through a 'dress rehearsal' with you. If the interviewer puts words in your mouth through the question – for instance, 'You've admitted liability for this oil slick, can you tell me what you are going to do about it?' – and this charge is misrepresentation, then gently correct them: 'Liability for the oil slick is still under investigation' or, more vigorously, 'I do not agree with the premise of your question; however, what I will say is ...' Some interviewers have a killer instinct for getting interviewees flustered: stand your ground and stay pleasant but firm. It is your manner people will remember more than the content of what you say.

On radio, make sure that you warm up your voice well, and listen to the questions. Before a TV appearance warm up your body, face and voice. Many an interviewee exposes tension through rounded shoulders or a clenched jaw. If you get an opportunity, watch the programme beforehand to familiarise yourself with the interviewer's style and the format. Think about the audience and what they will want to know. If you are going on daytime television to talk about what you do, then it is unlikely your audience will find it easy to identify with you if you are power-dressed in pinstripe and talk in jargon about your marketing strategy.

The technical apparatus and the self-important manner of many who work in the media can be daunting to a newcomer. If you don't know where to look, or what you cue is to speak, then ask. You could look a lot sillier later on if you don't. Avoid lots of distracting movements and blinking as a nervous reaction to studio lights (see the eye exercises in Chapter 4).

Brighter colours look good under studio lights. Avoid checks, dog-tooth and stripes, which can 'strobe' and look distracting. Wear something that you feel really comfortable in and which is appropriate for your image, the programme and the audience.

chapter eight

YOUR IMAGE AT WORK

W e all present a certain image of ourselves at work, and that image may be in some ways quite different from the images we have of ourselves at leisure with our family and friends.

We all present different facets of ourselves in different situations and with different people. The more adaptable you are, the easier these switches become. At work, it could be important to project an image of efficiency and competence; you and your colleagues will behave and present yourselves in a similar manner.

Adaptability, along with determination, is undoubtedly a key to success. At work you may need to adapt to different types of people, to greater responsibilities and to changes in job demands and different types of employers. Job fulfilment is very much to do with your needs being met: once more, balancing individual expression with the need for involvement with others is significant. In most jobs we need to adapt to and work well with others, but we also need the job to satisfy our self-image. Lack of recognition from superiors is cited as the most common cause of job dissatisfaction; the individual's contribution is not appreciated and so he or she does not feel particularly involved, or disposed to seek further involvement with the company.

The success or failure of a business or an organisation depends on the workforce. Companies are essentially about the people in them; success depends on employees' motivation to do their jobs well. Companies also have distinctive sets of values. In some businesses or organisations there will be a strong emphasis on caring and education and loyalty to the company. Staff will be encouraged to stay with the firm for many years. In other companies the emphasis will be on profit and personal achievement, and staff will often move on after several years. Often, too, different types of personalities will be employed in different jobs. A manager in the

PR department might be far more of an innovator than the conformist who is manager in the accounts department.

The more compatible your values are with the values of the company, the greater the likelihood of job satisfaction. In *Corporate Cultures* by Terence Deal and Allen Kennedy, the authors suggest: 'Values also play a very important role in determining how far one can rise within an organization. If product development is the company's overriding ethic, the best people will want to work in the company's research and development laboratories. If customer service is the important value, the go-getters won't want to be in finance but in a sales or field service function. The company will tend to reinforce the primacy of that value by promoting a disproportionate share of the people in these jobs.'

Sometimes people start to feel very uncomfortable with the image and role they project at work. If you feel that you are acting a great deal of the time, watching yourself doing this as a detached observer and not really believing the performance, then it could be time for a change. If you don't believe in your 'working image' then you will become unhappy and dissatisfied. Maybe you are working for a company where the business 'process' is far more important than the individuals working for the company. Many of the most successful companies have got that way because they have nurtured and developed their employees and this has been repaid by the loyalty and effort of the workforce.

Perhaps you are setting yourself unrealistically high standards, and constantly thinking that others are better than you, in which case you'll always be hearing that nagging, critical voice commenting on your performance. (This is an extremely common experience.) Talk about your feelings to a friend, and write down what other people at work would describe as your good qualities and ask yourself if all these virtues can be contained in one person. Very likely they can. But if there is a discrepancy between what your colleagues and you know to be your good qualities and what the job demands, then this feeling of being an 'impostor' could mean that you need to change jobs. You are probably trying too hard to fit a square peg in a round hole.

The image you project at work will be influenced by others around you, by how far you see yourself fitting in with them or wanting to establish a separate identity from them. Whether you are single-mindedly ambitious or, on the other hand, your job is simply a means of earning a living and you'd really rather be tending your allotment – it will show. You choose what attitudes and values you want to project, although these choices are not always consciously made. In this chapter, I'd like to consider how the way we behave and the way we present ourselves at work reflects these choices.

SPONTANEOUS SPEAKING

Most of the time we are speaking spontaneously, with little planning in advance. When we are to do this in front of a group of people it is called extemporaneous speaking. Of course, in ordinary conversation we are speaking spontaneously, too. When we speak in public we often take questions from the audience and here too we are speaking spontaneously, so much of the advice given in Chapter Seven applies. In meetings, interviews and presentations we also speak 'off the cuff'. Here are some tips to help you to remain relevant and fluent:

- Always ask yourself, what does my audience need to know? If you unexpectedly have to get up and speak in front of a group, think of the three most obvious questions they would like answered and go ahead and do that. When you are putting a case in meetings, or interviewing or being interviewed, the same thing applies. What do the others present need/want to know? If you put this in order of priority you have a clear structure and case.

- Limit the number of points you make; lists of three work very well and are readily assimilated by others. This is taught on most presentation courses and it has become almost a cliché to preface what you are going to say with 'Well, there are three main points'. Many politicians appear incapable of speaking without making repetitive use of this device.

- Your ending is more important than your beginning – it will stop you rambling on. Decide very quickly what to end with.

- Don't say too much. Make your points, then finish speaking.

- Take your time.

- Make plenty of eye contact.

- If caught 'on the hop' ask yourself what is my action (am I persuading, convincing, reassuring etc.)?

- The best exercise for inarticulateness when 'caught on the hop' is number 9 under breathing in Chapter Six (page 105); someone throws you topics, you pause, breathe, and then start talking off the top of your head. Get your partner or friend to call out work-related topics – topics that might be covered in a meeting, say – and start talking.

The Words we Use

Your skill with words can enhance your total image. People who have wide vocabularies, who always have the right word to describe exactly what they mean, are compelling talkers. Your vocabulary is affected by your linguistic ability, your level of education and how much and what you read. One of the most effective ways of improving vocabulary is to increase the amount that you read from the quality newspapers. Some of them have columns on the meaning and derivation of obscure and well-known words. Whenever you come across a word that you do not understand then look it up and learn it. Always carry a pocket dictionary.

A large vocabulary makes you more adaptable. It can help you express your message more precisely, and articulate your feelings so that they are better understood by others. A good command of language will make others regard you as someone who is intelligent and informed. You can adjust your language according to the people you are with: presenting to the board of directors you can use language that is appropriate to their status; when training a group of apprentices you can adapt your vocabulary so that you are clearly understood.

There are talkers and writers who like to use obscure words as a means of impressing people. Others, of course, have a genuine love of language, and of exploring its application. If someone uses a word that you don't understand, ask them what it means. Besides increasing your vocabulary, this may well dissuade the speaker who is deliberately using language to impress or mystify from continuing with this aim.

In the fields of information technology and finance in particular, jargon in the written and spoken word seems to be endemic. For those who understand the words, jargon is an effective shorthand. When you are talking to someone who is not familiar with the terminology and you are using a lot of jargon, it may sound again as though you are trying to impress or 'blind them with science'. When in doubt, use plain English.

The use of language indicates values in a culture. In America, where everyone 'lets it all hang out' rather more than we do, language is used in a suitably upfront manner: 'Have a happy day', 'I'm out of here'. In Britain language is used with considerably more restraint: 'How are you?', 'Excuse me, do you mind if I . . .' 'Would you mind awfully if I . . .'

Your use of language indicates your personal values, beliefs and priorities. If you are talking to someone and using words like 'goal', 'profit', 'lucrative', 'gain,' 'the bottom line', 'bankability', you will suggest different preoccupations than if you use vocabulary like 'insight', 'enlightened', 'aware', 'consciousness', 'sensitivity', 'spiritual'. Language can create strong, emotive association in others. The more you consider use of language and the wider your vocabulary, the less you risk offending, patronising or infuriating others.

Jack thought that other people seemed to find him aggressive. It was not his intention to be so, and he could not understand why. He was an authority on the history of furniture design and travelled the world lecturing on this subject. His audiences were often young and eager to hear what he had to say. In an attempt to break down imaginary barriers, Jack developed a habit of addressing groups of people as 'boys and girls'. First of all, he started using it to his audiences and then, as it became habitual, to address groups of more than two people. He had no idea just how alienating his use of language was; he thought he was sounding friendly.

Avoid use of forms of address such as 'dear', 'darling', 'love' or 'sweetheart' unless you are convinced the other person will appreciate it. For some groups, like some show-business people, these terms of address may be commonplace and widely reciprocated. But if you are not someone's 'dear' or 'darling' you may find this form of address extremely patronising. In which case, ask the person whether they would mind calling you by your name instead, or to make the point, start addressing them using a similar form. 'Pet' seems to be an effective one, to get the message over.

Sometimes people use language and association to demean others. For instance, if a boss said he liked your 'little report' and you had spent several weeks compiling that piece of work, you would justifiably feel put down. In this case, it may be worth pointing out gently that you were proud of your work, and that it had taken considerable time and effort on your part. I say do this gently, because very often apparent 'insults' are due to carelessness with language, rather than a deliberate snub.

Penny wanted to convince her boss that she needed two more people on her sales team. She prepared her case thoroughly, but kept peppering her statements with qualifying questions: 'Do you know what I mean?', 'You know?', 'Can you understand what I'm saying?', 'actually', 'in fact'. At the end of her case, her boss was far from convinced that *she* believed in what she was saying, let alone that he was persuaded of it. If you keep qualifying what you are saying and checking that others approve, you will not sound definite and confident. Women tend to do this far more than men.

Some speakers do the reverse. Rather than own up that a point of view is their opinion, they make the point sound as though it comes from a God-like authority. They use phrases like 'the fact is', 'there's absolutely no doubt', 'definitely,' 'as everyone believes'. This use of language can cause conflict. Far better, when something is your opinion to say 'in my opinion' or 'I'm of the view that'. Others will respect your honesty and not feel that you are imposing on them. Avoid too much use of 'one': it does not make it clear whether you are talking about yourself or everyone. Of course, the Royal Family use it and in bygone days it was not considered polite to say 'I' and 'me' too much. These days, though, the use of 'one' may be regarded as an affectation, and we are more direct in our communication.

Language changes with the times and slang, in particular, dates very quickly. If a man refers to females under forty as 'chicks' you may be sure that he was in his prime in the 1960s. Slang and 'in' words need to be used carefully. Bear in mind that slang words are most popular with adolescents, who are using language to establish and confirm their identity as part of a specific group.

It is widely agreed that people swear because their vocabulary is inadequate. We also swear to shock others, to show that we are not stuffy, to show that we do not care what others think and to appear tough and macho. Swearing is also a great way of letting off steam, when action could be a lot more destructive. The University of California found that people who swore were considered lower in intelligence and less attractive than those who did not. Swear words can, though, show allegiance with a group. When it is judiciously placed and unexpected, a swear word can have a powerful effect and grab the listener's attention.

LISTENING SKILLS

Many of us do not listen as well as we hear, and we forget that each of us has just one mouth but two ears through which to communicate. We assume that when we are not speaking we can switch off, not realising that listening is an active skill. To communicate well yourself, and to understand what others are communicating, you have to be able to listen. When we *hear* we acknowledge there is presence of sound, when we *listen* we interpret and process that sound. This is a skill that can make an immeasurable difference to how we come over in meetings, interviews and presentations as well as in day-to-day conversation. Great communicators are always great listeners.

It is possible to increase listening powers greatly. There are so many aspects to focus on when listening to someone talk: the speaker's breathing pattern, pitch, pace, clarity, volume and use and choice of language. Often we only hear what we want to, and what fits in with what we want to say next. By not receiving much of what is said, we limit the information we are getting about the speaker and the situation.

When you listen, you can perform many actions. You can analyse, fantasise, criticise, accept, reject, empathise, sympathise, approve, absorb, learn, etc. Poor listeners tend to be thinking of what they are going to say next, rather than receiving other people's messages. If you are under stress your listening ability can be impaired. You will be distracted by all the other messages, anxieties and fears that are overloading your brain. If you find yourself interrupting a lot, that is an indication that you are not a good listener. The other person will not feel at ease with you, and could decide that you are insensitive and aggressive. You don't have to bulldoze others to make your point. Men tend to interrupt women more than the other way round, and women, generally, are better listeners. In both sexes there are, of course, exceptions.

We watch each other listening. If you are listening and your body is twitching, you are drumming your fingers, yawning, letting your eyes wander, then your attention will be seen to be straying. Even though you might be attending, if you have a high degree of nervous tension and are using nervous mannerisms, then an averagely sensitive speaker will sense that you are not giving your full attention.

Any behaviour which indicates concern with yourself (fidgeting with your hair, your nails, adjusting your clothes), rather than attending to the speaker, is distracting. If you listen with defensive body language (arms crossed, hands in front of face) you will not appear particularly receptive. The best listeners forget about themselves and focus on what they are receiving. They are not concerned with creating an effect of listening, they are concentrating on the process and the means of conversation. They use steady, even eye contact, their faces will be relaxed, their body position open, and they will make little movement. Through nods of the head, 'mmns', 'I sees', 'yeses', they will indicate that they are absorbing what is being said and encourage the speaker to continue.

Exercises for Listening Skills

Here are some exercises to improve listening skills:

1. Take five minutes a day to sit quietly somewhere, close your eyes and

listen to all the sounds around you. Many people find this has a very calming effect.

2. When you are having a conversation with another person, receive what he or she has said before rushing in to make your contribution. If you instinctively butt in to make your point, think about pausing and breathing before you start to talk. A pause before you speak can also add an effect of significance.

3. Listen to the radio as much as possible, to plays, news programmes and discussions. Make decisions about what you have heard. What information did you receive and what impression did you form from different aspects of the broadcasters' speech?

4. To encourage others to continue talking, summarise or encapsulate what the speaker has said (in your own words): it shows that you have understood what has been said so far. So if someone explaining about next year's budget has just told you what the figure is, and you say 'So we have thirty per cent more than this year', they sense your interest and encouragement to continue.

5. With a colleague or friend, ask them to tell you about a problem they have at work or at home. If they are finding it difficult to talk, then it is up to you to encourage them. When they have divulged sufficient information, relate back to them what they told you. Ask them what you left out. This will indicate to you how you interpret messages and it should give you insight into what you choose to listen to, and what you ignore. Finally, ask your partner how well you listened and swap over.

In an ideal world, everything that we heard would be worth listening to. To be realistic, we often have to act as though we are listening, when someone is pontificating at length about something we already understand, for instance. Rather than switching off altogether in this situation, salvage what you can out of it. Use it to refine and develop your listening skills. You can always use the situation to study the signals that others send when they communicate.

COMMUNICATION BLOCKS

People have different talking 'styles'. Some people ask a lot of questions and see this as a means of gaining involvement. Others make far greater use of statements. If you are someone who favours the enquiring style, you may well find someone who tends to make statements unresponsive. As someone who favours making statements, you may find the person who asks questions intrusive.

Here are two contrasting examples in which A likes to ask questions and B prefers statements:

In this example **B** finds **A**'s questioning intrusive:

B: That was a tedious meeting.

A: Why? What happened?

B: There wasn't an agenda.

A: Oh dear, so what did you talk about?

B: Nothing much.

A: So what happened?

B: Um, nothing really . . .

Here **A** interprets **B**'s use of statements as reluctance to communicate.

A: That was tedious; what's happening?

B: Nothing much, phone's been going a lot.

A: Do you know they didn't have an agenda, can you believe that?

B: Yes.

A: We ended up not talking about anything. Have I missed anything?

B: The post came.

A: Oh, I see.

You need to consider that others may have a different conversational style from yours; again, it reflects how directly we seek involvement with others, or how much we wish to appear self-contained.

Other communication blocks include:

● *offering advice too readily*
When someone presents you with a problem they often want to use you as a sounding-board, rather than expecting you to come up with a ready-

made solution. You can appear to insult their intelligence and to be dismissive if you regularly offer instant solutions:

A: I'm a bit stuck over that meeting next week – I'm supposed to be working on my report that day.

B: Don't go to the meeting, I'll go instead.

A: Oh, I wasn't sure ...

B: Well, that's an easy way out, isn't it?

A: Uh, can I have a while to think about it?

- *being too judgemental*

If we fail to appreciate that others are different from us, and view them too much according to our own perspectives and prejudices, we can run into problems:

A: I'm not sure whether I can go to the meeting next week, I've got that report to do.

B: If I were you, I'd go.

A: Would you?

B: Yes, you're setting yourself too high a standard with that report, it doesn't need much more doing to it. Why are you so self-critical all the time?

A: I don't know.

- *avoiding other people's emotions*

Many of us feel uncomfortable when other people seem ill-at-ease, so rather than easing them into conversation about the problem, we change the subject or reassure them, not always realistically:

A: I'm not sure I can go to that meeting. I've got that report to do.

B: Oh you'll manage the report all right, nothing to worry about there.

A: But I don't think I can finish it in time.

B: Oh of course you will! Have you seen my black pen?

MEETINGS

Meetings take up a great deal of time in most of our working lives. A meeting is really any occasion when two or more people come together to talk, with some shared overall objective.

How can we present the best image of ourselves at meetings? Remember, there is no point in going to a meeting if you have nothing to contribute, and there is nothing to be gained by holding a meeting if the matter could be dealt with through memoranda. Wasting time is likely to make you and other participants feel irritable. We go to meetings to give and receive information and ideas, to persuade others, to agree upon a course of action and to find solutions to problems. It is always worth making some sort of positive contribution. So even if you disagree with what is being planned, be sure that you have an alternative course of action to suggest. Occasionally, people go to meetings just to make themselves heard and to sound off in a negative and destructive way. Those people rarely feel good about themselves at the end of the meeting.

It is important to prepare well for a meeting, if you know what is on the agenda. Decide what your objective is (why you are going) and what your means (actions) will be to achieve this objective. For instance, if your overall objective is to persuade your company to invest in marketing support (that is, using a marketing company) you could do the following:

- COMPARE your company's use of marketing support with that of rivals.

- JUSTIFY the need through projected profit increases.

- PRAISE the marketing company's record.

- DEMONSTRATE the possible growth using visual aids.

- CHALLENGE your company to try something new.

- AMUSE those present with your fervour.

- INVOLVE them by asking for questions from them.

These actions would be valid and effective ways of achieving your objective. When you focus on your actions, you prevent yourself becoming self-conscious and feeling inadequate or trying to be impressive or clever.

You'll avoid self-conscious behaviour, picking imaginary bits of fluff off your sleeve or talking in an affected, unnatural voice, for example. Prepare your case and arm yourself with statistics and correct information if you need it. Think about 'hidden agendas' – that is, the range of objectives that other people will be bringing to the meeting. If you understand why people are expressing certain views you are half-way to offering viable alternatives to them.

One of the most effective ways of getting your point of view accepted by a meeting is to communicate it in such a way that the other people present think they have come to a decision collectively. So, for example, rather than stating, 'I think we should accept this proposal', suggest that the meeting has a look at the proposal and makes a decision on it. Or if you want a budget cut, suggest: 'Have we thought about taking a look at the budget?' If you have proposals written out, it will help your case.

Asserting Yourself

Some of us have problems putting our messages over effectively. We find that, to make ourselves heard, we end up sounding emotional or angry. If you are having problems getting your message over, often simple calm repetition helps. The more you repeat a statement ('I don't want to go to that department'), the more others will appreciate that you are standing your ground. Take time to deliver your message, breathe in easily before you do so and let out the breath gently as you speak. That way the timbre of your voice will be steady and controlled and your pitch less likely to rise.

Make steady eye contact with everyone present, and pay particular attention to those who are browbeating or bullying you. If you are attacked or something makes you feel angry or upset, then voicing that feeling ('I feel angry' or 'I feel upset') will help you express your reaction in a reasoned way. If you repress your reaction, your behaviour (rather than what you say) may well give you away, and the messages you send will get confused: like the man who said 'No, that doesn't bother me at all' when questioned about a proposal. Only he made his reply through gritted teeth and with his eyes fixed firmly on the floor.

If someone is trying to interrupt you, increase the volume of your voice slightly and look directly at that person, without flinching. If they persist then indicate with your arm (a mini-version of the police traffic signal for 'stop' works well) that you wish to continue. At the worst, ask them in a very reasonable, calm, unhurried tone of voice, 'May I finish, then you can have your say' and continue with your point. Interrupters are poor listeners; remember *they* have the problem. When several people are trying to talk at once, it is often the person who persists in talking rather than the one who shouts loudest who eventually gets through.

Use your body language to help you get your point over: sit well back in the chair, with your back adequately supported, and keep your position open. I've already mentioned how 'steepling' – holding the hands together by linking the fingers – looks confident; when you are seated at a table you can 'spread' your territory by resting your arms on the table with the hands steepled, so that you create a half-circle of space in front of you.

Dressing for Meetings

Not only is your behaviour under scrutiny at meetings, but also your appearance. There is ample opportunity in most meetings for participants' attention to stray, and for them to make judgements about other people present. If in doubt as to what is appropriate to wear for a meeting, then it is always a good idea to wear a jacket. Especially if you are new in a job, you can look as though you are not taking the event or the other people seriously, if you turn up looking too casual. You are there to make a positive contribution and your clothes should help this. If you are particularly prominent, by virtue of your youth, sex, or 'newness' to the job then you will be a target of some interest, so dress with appropriate care and attention to detail.

Who Sits Where and When

A friend of mine works in a company with very little formality, where meetings go on for ever and very little gets achieved. She decided on drastic action: to announce at the outset of a meeting what needed to be resolved and to hold the meetings standing up. The transformation was astonishing. Decisions were made rapidly and the meetings ended quickly.

The timing of the meeting and where it is held matter. Early to mid-afternoon is known as the 'graveyard slot': most people are at their lowest ebb of energy and creativity, even if they haven't indulged in a heavy lunch. If you hold meetings at the end of the day, some participants will be thinking about what time they can get away, rather than the business in hand.

It makes sense to stipulate the length of time for a meeting, particularly if some of those present are especially voluble. In long meetings, you could choose to take breaks, for 'calls of nature', refreshment, to stretch your legs and allow brains to recharge.

If you are putting a case to a meeting, then you strengthen your side by holding the meeting on your territory. If that is not possible, then opt for neutral territory, rather than visiting the opposition.

The way we group in meetings is interesting and revealing. There is more equality in a meeting if everyone is seated around a table. If you have a visible head, at one end of a table or on a platform, then hierarchy is established. When there is a leader or a boss in the group, those who sit next to him or her almost always consider themselves 'next in line'.

If the meeting is being held around a rectangular table, and you sit in the middle of a long side, everyone will have a clear view of you when you make your contribution. You are in a more confrontational position if you sit opposite somebody. Allies will often sit side by side.

INTERVIEWS

For this section of *Your Total Image*, I talked to Sue Berry, of Insight Management Consultancy, who is an occupational psychologist and an expert on interview technique. Specific advice and tips from her appear at the end of this section.

Interviews are highly artificial situations which can have significant outcomes. In a relatively short period of time, far-reaching decisions can be made. Both interviewer and interviewee need to be adequately prepared: on both sides, it is a test of your total image and how well you project it.

Many interviewers fail to realise that they themselves are under scrutiny; with the predicted employee shortage and much more competition to get the best people, this attitude will need to change. The interviewer is the host, and must offer a welcome, take the visitor's coat if necessary, indicate a specific seat. Unless their intention is to intimidate, then they should smile, welcome the interviewee with a firm handshake and speak in a clear audible manner. If a CV has been sent in advance, the actual interview is not the time to read it.

The more accessible interviewee and interviewer are to one another in terms of positioning, the more receptive they can be to each other's physical signals. Desks and tables act as effective barriers. But an interviewee surrounded by a lot of space could feel vulnerable and exposed: a low coffee table nearby can make them feel more secure and provide a surface for papers and so on.

Sometimes an interviewer will sit in an upright chair and put the interviewee in a much lower seat. As an interviewee, regard this for what it is, an indication that the interviewer has to use seating as compensation

Interviewing with a barrier between.

Interviewing without a barrier.

163

for some inadequacy that he or she is feeling. As interviewer, you shouldn't talk too much, or wander off the subject. You don't need to oversell your company and its achievements, unless you lack the confident belief that people will want to come and work in it. If you are short of time, then it is unfair to show it and prevent the interviewee having a fair hearing.

Keep an open mind and you will find interviews very useful. If you only listen out for answers that you want to hear, then you could misjudge people. Interviewees will indicate a great deal about themselves, through the way they talk and what they say. The American furniture company called Herman Miller has as its company ethic: 'All people are extraordinary.' It is your job as interviewer to find out what makes each applicant extraordinary. A candidate may not be suitable for the marketing position that you wish to fill; but six months on when you are looking for a new personnel manager, he or she could be ideal.

At the beginning, you should let the candidate know the ground rules, how long the interview will last (you should be able to see a clock easily) and the sort of questions you will be covering. That way, you will not cause embarrassment if you suddenly start to ask probing personal questions. Your body language should be open and relaxed and you should signal encouragement, nodding your head and giving feedback to their answers. Open questions should make up the bulk of what is asked, rather than closed questions which simply require 'yes' or 'no' answers. Don't stick to set questions: you will limit the interviewees' opportunity to express themselves.

If you have not understood an interviewee's response, you can paraphrase what you think was said ('what you are saying is ...') to elicit clarification. If there are long silences it is your job to deal with them.

Many of us feel inadequate in some way as interviewees and so we may over-compensate by talking too much, disclosing more information about ourselves than is appropriate, answering a question in several different ways. You might be a keen collector of Victorian moustache cups, but it is unlikely that the interviewer will want to hear at length about your passion or that it will be relevant to the job (unless you are applying to work in a museum).

Think in advance about the main points that you want to make. Take your time to answer questions and if you feel nervous remember to pause and breathe. You can cover up and control nervous reactions: if your neck and chest go patchily red for instance, then wear something high-necked; if your palms are sticky, hold your wrists under the cold water tap to cool your hands down before you go in to the interview.

If you haven't understood a question, ask the interviewer for clarification. The way you answer the questions is very important.

J an was returning to work after raising a family. She felt that she was coming over as 'lightweight' in interviews. She smiled too much when she was nervous and when she responded to a question her voice lost energy at the end and went up in pitch. She sounded as though she was trying to ascertain whether she had finished or not. The impression this mannerism fostered was one of vagueness and lack of resolution. Interviewers found it difficult to know when to pick up on her replies and interviews were stilted and awkward.

When Jan learnt to curb her nervous smile and to answer questions so that they had definite, resolved endings her interview technique improved dramatically.

Don't rush to bring out a CV or examples of your work at the outset of the interview. It will indicate that you do not have confidence in your interview technique and that you are eager to provide a distraction from yourself.

The interviewer already has an assumed measure of power in the interview situation, and so it is unnecessary to 'power dress'. If anything, your appearance should be reassuring, and typical of a smart working outfit for your level in the company. For interviewees, the suit is accepted interview garb. In some professions, particularly creative business, it can be quite difficult to know how to dress. If you are really uncertain, you could make sure you pass the company building at nine a.m. or five p.m. and check out the 'dress code'. Your interview wear can then be a smartish version of this. Even within similar industries, employees can have a very different style. An American television programme, 'The Big Company' compared Apple Computers and IBM. Employees of the companies looked so different that it was inconceivable that they could have exchanged jobs without some radical alterations to their appearances, although they were all essentially working in the same industry. Apple employees favoured a casual, slightly 'alternative' look whereas IBM employees wore pristine business dress.

Here are Sue Berry's suggestions:

- Interviewees often do not prepare sufficiently, failing to TARGET WHAT THE ORGANISATION NEEDS TO KNOW. If you can research a company and come up with some key points from your experience that make you a suitable 'prospect', so much the better.

- Sometimes people over-prepare the words that they are going to use, so they sound like actors reciting a text. Very off-putting. Think about your ideas, rather than your lines.

- Many interviewees assume that they are better off talking in the abstract, probably from a sense that it is dangerous to commit yourself too much. When you can it is always better to give concrete examples. If, for instance, you are asked 'What do you think makes a good manager?' then you could answer by talking about management theory. Alternatively, and more effectively, you could relate back to your own experience 'As a manager, I've found ...' and give the interviewer an image of how you behave in that role. They can then start to visualise you as a manager at work, and you are that much nearer the interviewer constructing an image of you doing the job that is on offer.

- You are certainly judged on your appearance. Don't look too extreme and remember the 'people like us factor'. Err on the understated side. Steady eye contact is most important and you want to be 'alert but relaxed'.

- You present a heightened version of your total image at interviews in the same way as you do when you are speaking in public. Your speech needs to hold more interest than most of us use during normal conversation. Talk in shorter sentences than feels usual rather than long, meandering ones. You will make your points more clearly.

- We tend to regard interview questions like examinations. When we are asked something we respond to show everything we know about the subject. 'Leave them wanting more' is what you should think. The interviewer gets interested and has scope to ask you further questions, making the interview flow smoothly. As Sue said: 'Nothing turns an interviewer off more than somebody moving into their sixth paragraph.'

- It is important to establish right at the outset what is going to be covered in an interview. Interviewees are vulnerable and often therefore suspicious; if they are worried that they are being manipulated then their performance will suffer.

- Interviewers are attracted to interviewees who are like them. This is unfair but true. However, you will also make a strong impression if you have done your homework, if your manner matches what you say and, above all, if you have a constructive, positive approach. Most people can do more to improve the way they present themselves.

THE TELEPHONE

Many of us have to use the telephone to such an extent that it is worth giving some time and consideration to making the best of the medium.

Your 'speaking image' will never be effective if you do not like the sound of your voice, so if you would like to alter your sound, then read Chapter Six of this book and seek professional help.

British Telecom have published some recommendations regarding the use of the phone. If you want to sound powerful and decisive, or you have to assert yourself, stand up to make the call. We use energy differently when we stand from when we sit; if you're having a long, relaxed chin-wag with a chum you'll be more comfortable sitting down and you'll sound more relaxed. When we stand we often feel more assertive and decisive, so standing to make phone calls can make us sound more positive.

Earlier on in this book I mentioned 'right-brain' and 'left-brain' thinking. The right-hand side of the brain is said to control intuition and imagination, the left-hand side, logic and structured thinking. According to the BT psychologist, if you speak on the phone listening with your right ear, then you will 'tune in' and create greater empathy with people, but on the other hand (or should I say 'ear'?) if you want to make a logical case or structured proposition, then you are better off using your left ear.

When you suggest something to somebody over the phone, it is a good idea to put the suggestion that you would like them to accept last. This is because we are, it seems, a bloody-minded lot, and we assume that the first suggestion made is the one the speaker wants us to accept, so we usually go for the second one. If you are answering the phone a great deal, it is easy to sound tired and bored. A smile can help and bring a pleasant tone to the voice. Visualising whom you are speaking to can also help bring your message alive. If you habitually drop or raise your head at an angle to speak on the phone, then you could be putting pressure on your voice. Slumping while on the phone, as well as damaging your posture and making you look older and fatter, will also dampen the energy level and brightness in your voice. Always speak with your head at a comfortable angle, with the neck and head relaxed. If your voice gets tired, use more articulation rather than tensing in the throat.

A great many service businesses are almost entirely reliant upon how employees sound on the phone. It is important, I think, if you are answering the phone to clients or customers, to sound relaxed and warm. Although you might be fraught and very busy, do not allow this to affect your phone manner. Breathe out slowly as you reach to pick up the receiver and take your time to say your number, company name and/or your name.

If you tend to speak quickly, or your pitch rises when you get excited, or you mumble, then stick a notice on the phone to remind you about this habit. If you get wound up, you need a sign saying 'relax' on the phone. Listen carefully and if you find that you are always asking people to repeat information, then have your hearing checked and do the listening skills exercises given earlier in this chapter.

Some companies have set ways of answering the phone: 'Hello this is 1234567, Smooth Operator. This is Mary speaking, how may I help you?' That's fine, provided the speaker does not sound robotic. Many companies fail to realise how important that first phone contact is and how often the phone is answered by someone who sounds bored and uninterested. The phone should be answered by someone who invites you in and makes you feel welcome, with a manner and sound that makes you feel you can trust them and that they deserve your business.

Some people are phone phobics and spend as little time as possible on the line. They are often charming, loquacious individuals when you meet them in the flesh, but on the phone they are abrupt and brisk. They are likely to be people who rely a lot upon visual clues to determine the way they communicate and they can benefit from making themselves more comfortable with just listening. If you have 'phone phobia' relax yourself before you make a call, get yourself in a very comfortable position (reclining on a sofa, maybe – even lying in the bath) and close your eyes to focus entirely on the call and nothing else. Take your time and breathe. Make yourself relax and enjoy conversations with your nearest and dearest over the line.

It is assertive to take the initiative in making a phone call, rather than waiting for someone to call you if you are in doubt as to which party is to make the call. Busy people may have difficulty finding time to return calls, but some people choose not to return calls as a way of creating distance, and making themselves appear powerful. This isn't a very courteous way to behave.

If you have an answering machine then decide for what purpose. If you want people to leave messages, then try to sound warm and reassuring. Many people still dislike answering machines; either they don't like the sound of their voices, they dislike what they regard as the 'permanent' nature of leaving a message, or they don't like talking to irresponsive machines. Gimmicky recordings can be very irritating; especially if the caller has to listen to them frequently.

YOUR CV

A CV is often the first contact employers have from you and it should be well presented with your relevant work experience prominent. Don't be negative, apologetic or humorous and gimmicky unless you understand the humour of the people who are receiving it. Even then, they might not consider an application to work in their company as a joking matter. Think about your own qualifications, experience and interests and sieve through them once more to TARGET WHAT THE ORGANISATION NEEDS. Edit your achievements so that you present them in the best light for the particular job that you are after. It is far better to have less information on a CV but for it all to be relevant, than to fill your CV with detailed examination results that you got twenty years ago.

If you have been working a long time, then it is best to start with your most recent employer and work backwards. As a relative newcomer to the job market, you would be better off starting with your education and then working forward. The first structure puts emphasis on your experience, while the second emphasises your achievements.

To have your CV professionally prepared, go to a recommended company.

SOCIALISING AT WORK

When you are involved in work-related socialising, you are still conducting business. Your behaviour and clothes should reflect this. Go for tailored clothes and if you are attending an informal event, dress 'smart but casual'. Choose evening dress that is tailored, but in 'evening' fabric. You will only confuse your colleagues and cause speculation about your reliability if you 'let your hair down' in either the way you behave or dress. This is particularly important for those on the lower rungs of a career ladder.

Learn to make small talk. It is an underestimated skill and one that is very useful. It indicates to the other person that you are happy to be in their company and that you have common areas of understanding. Choose topics that everyone can talk about: the event itself, the surroundings, a news story, transport. Listen and encourage the other person to talk. Avoid boasting, strong criticism, and revealing too much about yourself early on in the conversation. Small talk can often lead on to bigger issues, and is a good way of finding out whether you are compatible enough with someone to do business together.

chapter nine

YOUR WORKING ENVIRONMENT

To what extent do your surroundings enhance or detract from your total image? If you have your own business and your work often involves visiting people on their territory, then the fact that your office is a dingy back bedroom need not jeopardise your chances of success. Your behaviour, appearance and voice will be far more important. That gloomy office could be detrimental to your attitude towards your work, however. It could tempt you to spend far too much time visiting people and not enough time back at base, thinking and planning. If your clients and customers visit you, then the surroundings in which they see you will be very important.

Even in a smart, modern building, you could well have other distractions to contend with. In open-plan offices there is often noise and distraction from other people, making contemplative work difficult. In a large company, the uniformity and strict specification of the design of your office could add to your feeling of being a very small cog in a very large wheel.

Aspects of the working environment can exert detrimental influences over how we feel and therefore the total image we project. In this chapter, I would like to look at the signals we send out to others through our surroundings, and how we ourselves are affected by them. I shall also consider your 'corporate' image, how to project the appropriate image when you work at home, and how your 'trappings', like choice of notepaper, can reinforce the impression that you want to create.

WHAT YOUR SURROUNDINGS COMMUNICATE

How much time do you spend in your workspace? Many of us spend more time in the office than we do in our living rooms or kitchens and yet we give a fraction of the time and consideration to thinking about where we work as compared to where we cook or watch television.

Our surroundings can affect our attitude towards our work and how well we feel when we are there. Working in a pleasant airy office with plenty of light and space feels very different from working in dark cramped dingy surroundings. Comfortable working conditions can affect both our psychological and physical well-being.

For this chapter, I sought the advice of Elaine Clerici, of Clerici Design Consultants. Your working environment, Elaine thinks, 'should say something about your business, not you'. You can over-personalise your workspace; you could be really proud of your yachting or hockey trophies, but visitors need to see that you are good at your job rather than having your expertise at sport forced on their attention.

When you make a grand visual display of your achievements, in a sense you intrude on your visitor's senses. Many of them will find it necessary to comment on the trophies, and in the ensuing conversation you will be able to confirm rapidly what the trophies indicate. You are blatantly displaying skills in a way that can overpower others. There will be no opportunity for your visitor to say to you, further on in your relationship, 'Oh, so you're a keen yachtsman/hockey player?' There is no sense of quiet confidence in an achievement when evidence of it is spread all over your surroundings. Also to others, the blatant display can seem like overpowering self-promotion.

Your surroundings can reflect your main intentions in your work. As someone who works in advertising, for instance, you might want to make a strong statement about the creative nature of your work through your 'setting'. You will be using settings and backgrounds to send out signals about your client's products and so it would be appropriate that your own 'setting' boldly sends out signals about you. You could choose a moody, fashionable interior, with low lighting, modern designer furniture and prominent abstract art.

One of the main questions to ask is: 'Who will be coming here?' As a young solicitor who does a lot of divorce work, then your clients could often be distressed and confused. Your priorities could be to create an atmosphere that is reassuring and reliable. In your surroundings you could choose to do this through well-worn antique furniture, traditional prints on the walls, comfortable squashy leather chairs. On the other hand, if you represent a large number of 'arty' people, writers and designers, you might go for a less traditional and more creative look, indicating an empathy with your clients. You could choose to have a 1930s or 1950s influence in decor and furniture, if that appealed to your taste.

We expect certain atmospheres from different professions. If I went to a dentist who had a brightly-coloured waiting room and played heavy metal music through the stereo system, I doubt whether I would remain a patient for long. When we go to see someone for professional services, then we expect a suitable professional-looking environment and our confidence will be undermined by chaotic, dirty surroundings.

We see 'settings' used to great effect on television and in advertising and the background against which we are portrayed can reinforce or contradict what we are saying:

A right-wing political spokesman was featured on a late night news programme, commenting on a topical issue. He was filmed on the staircase of an interior (presumably a Conservative club) with a large photograph of Winston Churchill behind him. Before he opened his mouth, the viewers would have made all sorts of judgements about this man. He had been set up by the programme maker to represent an extreme point of view and the background was being used to do this most effectively.

It isn't just the inside of the building that matters, either. In some professions, having 'the right address' is very important. If both location and interior are miserable, then the combination can be most detrimental:

Keith had been approached by Deirdre to become a partner in her marketing business. He had enjoyed his dealings with her on previous occasions, and thought her a good businesswoman who presented herself well. She was well-groomed, intelligent and articulate. Keith only had one qualm; he wasn't sure whether he trusted Deirdre. She took him out for an expensive lunch to make her proposal and suggested that Keith visit her office for a day, to see what he thought. Deirdre's offices were quite awkward for him to get to; he couldn't drive because traffic and parking were difficult, so he had to use public transport. This didn't bother Keith particularly; he suspected that the out-of-the-way location of the offices meant that they would be especially pleasant. He was wrong. The offices were dingy, poorly decorated, inadequately heated and Keith would have been working in the same room as Deirdre and subject to her continual interference. Although Deirdre's company was successful and she employed twelve people, her offices confirmed Keith's fears: that Deirdre was not all that she appeared to be on the surface and that she was not a considerate employer. He turned down her job offer.

This story illustrates several points. You could argue that as Deirdre did not have clients visiting her office, the decor did not matter. (She usually met them in hotels in central London.) The interior, however, was not conducive to morale and could have been easily and cheaply improved by giving the greyish walls a coat of white or cream paint. Perhaps Deirdre was just not 'surroundings-conscious', and indeed some people do not seem to be much affected by their environment. Unfortunately, in a business (marketing) where the 'look' of things really matters, she needed this awareness. The signals she sent out through her sophisticated appearance were at odds with the signals sent out by the dingy background and 'read' to Keith as inconsistencies.

We can't control how much people 'read' into our surroundings and so it makes sense to make our environment pleasant and practical for ourselves and for visitors. Personality type, of course, comes into this; introverts require far less outside stimulation than extroverts and so where an introvert might choose a quiet restful environment, with clean simple lines, an extrovert could choose brighter colours and bold paintings, furniture and objets d'art.

Some of us require order in our environment far more than others and certainly if orderliness is an important factor in your work, then 'creative chaos' in the office would not inspire confidence. A solicitor or accountant needs to look as though he or she has the paperwork organised or under control, and not necessarily on display. On the other hand, if you went to a design studio or a publishers where there was no paper or manuscripts lying around, you might well wonder whether they had any commissions or were working on any books. That's not to say that creativity and chaos are interdependent; some highly creative people can only work in very tidy surroundings, while others feel ideas flow more freely when they are surrounded by comforting clutter.

If you work for a large corporation, then the control you have over your surroundings could well be regulated and restricted. Companies like IBM commission extensive research into the design of workspace and use the results to standardise space and furniture. Sometimes the office designers provide very little scope for the individual to personalise his or her 'space'; if you are lucky you might have the odd notice board on which you can pin things. Over-regimentation and restriction in workspaces can contribute to making employees feel like faceless 'corporate clones' and that they, as individuals, have little contribution to make. In some instances, you might not want to personalise your office, because you are just 'passing through' and do not intend staying at that company for any length of time. In some companies space is strictly commensurate with status; the higher your title the bigger your office. Window space can also be status linked, corner offices and *two* windows being strictly reserved for top cats only.

When we meet someone for the first time and they start to tell us all their personal problems, we feel embarrassed. In the same way, if someone's office is overpoweringly personal and they disclose a great deal of information about themselves, we feel awkward. Take Erica, for instance:

E rica was a senior manager in an organisation who had booked me to do a couple of days' training. When she invited me into her office, I had a problem preventing myself gasping. It was full of forty or fifty soft toys – teddy bears, pandas, etc. The office itself was large and airy, with a big window and a lovely view. This was just as well, because I was able to comment on the view and stare fixedly out of the window, instead of eyeing the menagerie. I could only speculate as to how Erica could exert authority in this office. When I later returned to do another training course with the same group, they informed me that they had ousted Erica as course director and were now running the training themselves. A very easy coup, if the zoo was anything to go by.

Let's take a look at what specific features of our surroundings can communicate:

Reception Areas

- Large companies often have enormous reception areas so that the scale and power of the company is impressed upon visitors. This can make a visitor feel dwarfed, insignificant and vulnerable, especially if there is little furniture about. This exposure means that the company's employees can scrutinise you easily and see that you are not an obvious security risk.

- Reception areas are the first aspect that visitors see. Unless you want actively to discourage visitors, the more welcoming the environment the better.

- Achievements, certificates, examples of your work make effective displays in a reception area. They give visitors something to look at, something to talk about when they meet you and they can help establish your credentials. Displays are a cheap and effective means of self-promotion.

- Many companies favour low, squashy chairs in reception areas. These work well in a dentist's waiting room, where they can make you feel floppy and relaxed. Most visitors, though, will have gone to those companies and organisations with a definite purpose and the feeling of sitting in a low, soft chair works against that intention. Far better to have chairs that give better support with a more 'up' feeling, so that visitors' purpose, body language and body positioning can be compatible.

- Visitors will feel happier waiting with a visual focus: plants, flowers, a fish tank, paintings, sculpture. Coffee tables with magazines also provide distraction and protection.

- Allocate as much as you can from your budget to making the reception area attractive. If visitors are waiting there, they will have already formed a distinctive impression of you and your business before they meet you and visit your office. The reception area should clearly show what the business is about.

Offices

- Once in the office, if you do not have a reception area as such, it shows consideration for your visitors to provide somewhere for them to hang their coats.

- Office decor needs to be functional and subtle. Dark, warm colours make rooms look smaller, and light, cool colours make them look bigger. North-facing windows make rooms colder and the light is cooler; south-facing windows make rooms correspondingly warmer in terms of sunlight and heat. To create a feeling of space, stick to light, cool, neutral colours.

- Green walls can create a relaxing atmosphere, perhaps *too* relaxing for work. (In hospitals, wards, operating theatres and surgeons' gowns are often green.)

- The light reflected by certain shades of yellow can make people look ill and jaundiced.

- Depressed people often decorate rooms entirely in white, showing a craving for outward order.

- Herman Miller, the American furniture-maker, believed that the most prominent aspects of rooms should be the people in them, not the walls or the furniture.

- Freshly painted walls are a relatively cheap way of giving your workspace a facelift.

- Always consider decor in terms of the natural light available and the artificial light that will be used. Rooms facing north, for instance, will have a colder natural light than those facing south.

Lighting

- Lighting can add interest to a stark, functional room. If you have only a central ceiling fitting, the spread of light will be uniform and dull. Create interest in rooms by lighting work areas and highlighting features.

- Lighting can affect the colour of the walls, the colour of the furniture and how well people look in the office. If you want a very stark, cool-looking office and you paint your walls white and then light them with a warm tungsten light you will not achieve the desired effect. In the same way, if you want a warm effect and have painted the walls cream, fluorescent tubing will work against your intention.

- Fluorescent lights tend to give off a cold, harsh, draining light, but you can buy diffusers for some types. These lights can create a strong, clear light for a workspace, provided that you buy the best quality. It is a good idea also to have desk lights to create relief. The newer halogen lights give off a much warmer, softer light, which is kinder on the eyes and the surroundings. They are more expensive than tungsten or fluorescent types, but their effect is well worth the investment.

- If you focus light on attractive features like plants and paintings, visitors are less likely to notice the damp patch near the ceiling or the frayed carpet.

- If you work in a large company where offices are standardised, you can add distinction and comfort to your office by taking in your own choice of desk light.

- The more natural light available the better. Even a small, cramped office can seem roomier if it has a large window with a lot of natural light.

- Since the discovery of Seasonal Affective Disorder (SAD for short, and it makes people feel that way) which affects sufferers in the winter because of the lack of natural light, lighting manufacturers have started making spectrum lighting which is a very close imitation of natural light.

The Atmosphere

Turn-offs for visitors

- Too much heat and stuffiness.

- Lots of background noise.

- Phones ringing and constant interruptions.

- Heaps of clutter on your desk – very distracting.

- Uncomfortable furniture, low chairs that women, in particular, have difficulty sitting on in a dignified manner.

Turn-ons for Visitors

- Obvious places for them to put briefcases and coats and to sit down; diversions for them to focus on if they are kept waiting.

- Quiet classical music at reception can create a soothing ambience.

- Focal points for them to look at in the office, e.g. plants and flowers.

- Sitting at an angle to a direct light source: head on it feels as though you are being interrogated.

- Offices that are a comfortable temperature and well-ventilated.

- Estate agents suggest that the smell of freshly brewed coffee helps sell houses; it also smells good in the office. If you don't want you or your visitor to get wound up, make it decaffeinated. It is considerate to have tea or mineral water available, too.

On a Budget

Elaine made several suggestions for those of us creating a workspace on a budget. She suggested:

- Co-ordinate the decor in basic neutral colours that are easy to match (creams, whites, greys).

- Choose modern, versatile furniture and fittings that are functional and cheap.

- Spend proportionately less on decor and furniture and buy one special item; a light, desk or chair that is impressive and eye-catching. If money is very tight, then choose a spectacular plant. Make this the focal point of your office.

A HEALTHY WORKPLACE

Recently experts have identified another illness of the 1980s: Sick Building Syndrome. Your workplace can make you sick – literally. Symptoms include catarrh, skin allergies, headaches, backache and blurred vision. As many as eight out of ten office workers in central London complain of ill health and adverse effects caused by the environment in which they work. One health centre in central London has a course of treatment aimed specifically at this complaint. Employers are increasingly becoming aware of how 'sick' buildings can affect productivity and profit.

However, employees are less affected by environmental factors than by psychological ones. In *The Social Psychology of Industry* J. A. C. Brown suggests that: 'The morale of the worker (i.e. whether or not he works willingly) has no direct relationship whatsoever to the material conditions of the job. Investigations into temperature, lighting, time and motion study, noise and humidity have not the slightest bearing on morale, although they may have a bearing on physical health and comfort.' He goes on to describe a team who worked with joy and enthusiasm in dismal conditions in a London slaughterhouse and protested strongly when it was suggested that the team be split up so that the individuals within it could work in much improved surroundings. Morale is definitely boosted by a good working environment; but a positive attitude to work will not be generated by environment alone.

Job satisfaction can be increased by pleasant, healthy surroundings and your working environment should help you to enjoy your work and project your total image effectively. If you are sweating profusely because of an overheated office, or slumping because of a badly designed chair, then it will be difficult to send out positive signals.

For someone who is feeling a lack of control in other areas of their lives, irritation and discomfort in the environment will aggravate the stress they are experiencing:

Tony was building up his own business, a training company, and working very hard to do so. One of his clients changed the venue of a course, which meant that he had a two-hour drive to get there, rather than the usual 45 minutes. When he got to the venue, a hotel, they were having major structural renovations, and the reception area and most of the hotel were full of scaffolding and workmen. This incensed him out of all proportion to its inconvenience factor; he saw these disrupted surroundings as the final straw and grumbled at length about them to the course organiser. Certainly the surroundings were not conducive to people's enjoyment of learning: most people on the course obviously wanted to go home as soon as possible. They also had more cause to grumble than he did – they were staying in the hotel. A few days later he was able to laugh at his over-reaction, but his session did not go well for him or his trainees.

If you are suffering from itchy sore eyes, back, head, or neck ache or catarrh; if your skin is irritated or you get tense or anxious at work, then factors in the environment could be contributing towards these symptoms. Here are some contributory factors:

Noise

We get excited and aroused by loud music with a rapid rhythm; quiet, soothing classical music can have the opposite effect. When we are in company, the music that stimulates and energises one person will make another feel agitated and irritable, depending on how each individual responds to external stimuli. If you work in an environment where there is a lot of mechanical noise, then you could find that music in the background will dampen the sound of the machines and distract from it.

In open-plan offices it is not easy to get away from noise of others working. A few years ago, open-plan offices were embraced as a great idea; employers discovered that they were cheaper to heat, light and floor, and bosses could keep an eye on the workforce. The arrangement could encourage communication between employees and help them work as teams. Nowadays the disadvantages have become apparent: constant noise, lack of privacy and the feeling of being relentlessly 'watched', difficulties in doing any sort of contemplative work. We are seeing a return to separate offices or a mixture of these with open-plan areas, according to function.

Some considerate employers will house all the noisy machinery in one room. Where this is not possible and you have to work with constant background noise, there should be provision of a 'quiet area'; somewhere you can get away from all the sound. In open-plan offices, screens can muffle sounds, and you can buy pads for typewriters and hoods for computer printers which serve the same function. Some office equipment manufacturers make boxes to enclose equipment and cut down noise. Textured surfaces absorb sounds better than smooth ones (which is why singing in the bathroom produces such a clear, bright sound), so you could want to revive the sixties fashion of hessian walls. Many of us find phones with buzzers less startling than those which have bells.

If noise is really getting to you, and your boss allows it, you can always wear a personal stereo playing some Mozart or use a pair of ear plugs!

For many of us these suggestions are impractical; in which case we should try to spend our lunch hours and breaks in a quiet, soothing atmosphere to avoid the relentless noise causing a stress build-up. When this is impractical, make sure that you set time aside at home for a peaceful 'wind-down'.

Heating and Ventilation

Some very serious problems can occur through pollution of the atmosphere at work. Under the Health and Safety at Work Act, certain regulations govern such hazards. You may want to contact your local town hall to get in touch with an environmental health inspector, or call in a Health and Safety Executive inspector from the Civil Service, if there is a severe problem. Alternatively if you are a member of a union, they may be able to advise you and take up your case.

When an office is poorly ventilated, the occupants can suffer from headaches, catarrh and lethargy. Air conditioning systems can be difficult to clean, which can sometimes result in the air becoming polluted. The atmosphere can become charged with too many positive ions, from heating, air conditioning and computers. Ionisers, which pump out negative ions, can help clean up the atmosphere. Machinery and substances used at work can give off chemicals which can irritate the skin or eyes and cause allergic reactions. If an ioniser has been in a room for some period of time, the skirting boards and corners of the room will be covered with a fine black dust, tangible evidence of the pollution.

If central heating is making the air very dry, then you could want to put humidifiers on the radiators, or place bowls of water under the radiators. (Humidifiers can also help to prevent wood splitting in antique furniture.) Plants can also help keep the atmosphere clean; spider plants in particular oxygenate the atmosphere.

Lighting and Computer Screens

It makes sense to have adequate light in your workspace. If you find the light harsh and tiring, rather than cutting down on the amount of light used you probably need to redistribute it in different forms. Shiny surfaces reflect glare, so if you are working under harsh fluorescent light in front of a VDU screen for long hours, you could get headaches and sore eyes. Computer screens give off low levels of radiation; and some experts recommend that pregnant women should avoid prolonged exposure to them. Screens are available which are said to protect from this radiation. If you are working with overhead fluorescent light, then you could want to get the light fitted with a diffuser. Alternatively, and most effective in my opinion, get yourself an uplighter giving adequate but indirect light. You can also buy desk lights specially designed for computer screens. Take hourly breaks away from the screen, to relax and moisten your eyes.

Furniture

When choosing a computer, it make sense to buy one that has a separate screen and keyboard, so that levels can be adjusted according to height of the person and desk. The screen should be at or just below eye level. Your chair and desk can help your posture indicate a positive attitude.

Desk level often needs to be lower than we think. You should be able to sit comfortably with your forearms at right angles to your body when they are on the desk. A chair with a high back will provide better support than a low one, and will provide essential support for the small of your back. Back problems can be caused by sitting badly, and many of us spend a great part of our working day at our desks. If you are plagued by back problems it is well worth investing in a specially designed chair to help you sit well. They are available from specialist shops catering for people with bad backs.

SPACE AND TERRITORY

The amount of space we like to be surrounded by is determined by personality and culture. We all walk around within 'bubbles' of personal territory. Positioning yourself too close to another person can be seen as intimidating and invading rather than conveying the friendly closeness you intend.

Confident, self-possessed people look easy surrounded by space. They do not need to cling to furniture or to stand very close to groups when they talk to them. Standing or sitting surrounded by a lot of space we are vulnerable and exposed; if we look unthreatened and non-defensive in this space we appear self-assured and powerful. This is why it is important if you are welcoming a visitor or an interviewee to your office, that you should give them specific directions as to where to sit, rather than let them flounder in space.

The way we use space can be an indication of our attitudes. People who enter a room and spread their possessions around it, then flop out in a chair taking up plenty of space, show that they feel at ease and that they belong in this territory. On the other hand if someone sidles into a room and sits neatly in a corner, they are showing that they are on less familiar ground and that they do not want to be particularly obtrusive. The same thing applies to entering another person's office; if you hang around the door you will look tentative and apologetic, but if you move purposefully to the centre of the room you look as though you have a right to be there.

A very cluttered environment launches an assault on the senses; a very clinical, ordered environment can make it very difficult for a visitor to relax. Of course, our responses to these conditions depend on our individual personalities and whether we are attracted by stimulus or order.

From a practical viewpoint, if you are a tidy, ordered person, you will be more successful at keeping paperwork and files hidden away; having a sense of 'a place for everything' you will keep your cupboards and filing cabinets tidy. If, on the other hand, you have to make a conscious effort to be tidy, they you might be better off keeping paperwork and files on display and sorting through them and throwing out at regular intervals.

Lack of space can be stressful. If you travel to work on an overcrowded tube and then work in an overcrowded open-plan office, you could end up feeling physically and psychologically cramped. Sometimes you might need to create your own space by rearranging your desk so that it excludes others. it is most important to establish an adequate work area, which is your territory. Relocation agencies who help senior executives find new jobs recognise that one of the most traumatic effects of losing a job can be that you have no workspace where you 'belong'. Therefore they provide their clients with a working area, with a desk and chair where the clients can research and prepare CVs and job applications. We need our space.

At work, amount of space and size of furniture can be equated with status. The most revealing and open interactions occur when both parties are seated without any barriers between them on equal-sized chairs, so that they can both see each other's body at a similar level.

If there is available space, it is worth creating a separate seating area for meetings and interviews, away from your desk. Seating arrangements can also influence interaction: it is more confrontational to sit directly opposite someone and more intimate and friendly to sit alongside. It has been suggested that if you want to disarm someone and make them an ally then you help your cause by sitting alongside them.

WORKING FROM HOME

I'm including this topic in *Your Total Image* because, according to the Henley Centre for Forecasting (which predicts social change), the number of people who work from home is going to increase dramatically. In my experience, working from home does pose certain problems in terms of projecting an image; most of us behave and dress differently at home from when we go to an office, and if we have visitors to our 'home' office they need to arrive in surroundings that are conducive to business.

Working from home has some great advantages, and technological advances mean that increasing numbers of people are able to work in this way. Gone for them are the horrors of commuter travel and, in many cases, the rigid nine-to-five routine. The home office can make it easier to combine a job and family life. However, it must be made clear to the family that you need time and space for your work. You will gain in avoiding the hectic nature of city life, but you will need to cultivate self-discipline and establish your work as top priority. For many people it helps to work set hours, expecially when they first start working from home.

We tend to take the companionship that we get from working with others for granted. If you spend a great deal of your time alone at a desk you can begin to feel isolated and out of touch with the rest of the world: in that case it is worth planning activities that get you out of your office and bring you into contact with other people. Working from home can also be detrimental to your physical fitness – after all, you don't get much exercise walking to work to the basement or the attic. You might need to build a regular exercise routine into your working week.

The Henley Centre for Forecasting also predicted that the growth in the numbers of home workers will mean an increased demand for certain goods, such as office equipment for the home and stylish leisure clothing. I think it helps to have a workmanlike attitude if you make some sort of effort to present yourself for work, even if you are spending all day alone. You'll feel more effective if you groom yourself as though you were going to the office, even though your clothes may be more casual. You could well find that you make a definite distinction in your wardrobe between the casual clothes that you wear in your home office and the smart tailored clothes you wear for meetings and trips out.

If you hold meetings in your home office, it is worth considering the attitude of the people attending those meetings. Some people can hold prejudices that a business run from home must be lacking in professionalism in some way. When my company Voiceworks first started seeing clients in our 'home office' (the kitchen) we were aware that our surroundings hardly enhanced the aura of professionalism we wanted to project. So my partner and I would get ourselves up in severe business suits to try to compensate for the environment. This strategy didn't work; the contrast between the way we looked and our surroundings only made both appear incongruous. We were trying too hard.

Many commuters find the idea of working from home a very attractive one, so that a prejudice against home-based business is often tinged with envy. Some people will be more nervous than if they were attending a meeting on the more neutral ground of an office. Going to someone's house for a meeting makes the whole event a lot more personal: you are a guest on their territory and to an extent your behaviour will need to reflect your 'visitor' status. If it is difficult to assert yourself in someone's office, it is doubly difficult to do so in their home. There are other reservations, too, that we can feel when we go and see someone about business in their home. Because our homes disclose far more about us than an office, you are likely to form a strong first impression of the host and also to learn far more about him or her than you would in an office situation. You might not like what you see.

There are ways in which as a 'homeworker' you can help dispel your visitors' reservations and prejudices. If you make your behaviour as businesslike as possible, while being welcoming and pleasant, you will set the tone for the meeting. Most of us associate going to someone else's house with social behaviour so it is easy to become confused. If you wear a kaftan to receive a first-time visitor then this will reinforce the difference between your world and theirs. You could be better off wearing a casual tailored jacket, a 'soft' version of business dress, which could help create greater affinity between you and your visitor.

The more you can separate your office from the rest of the house, the better. When you decide where to have your home office, it is worth remembering that you are likely to spend more time in that room than any other. If you can, choose a room or an area with plenty of natural light. If you can position your desk so that it faces a window, so much the better.

The rest of the family need to understand that this is your territory; and even if you have to use the kitchen table as your office, you could want to screen off the area to help define its function.

The extent to which your workspace looks like a functioning office or an extension of your home depends on the sort of work you do and your taste. It also depends on whether you are going to be using the office for anything else: letting the office double up as a guest room could end up being highly inconvenient, but if it doubles up as a study for the rest of the family then it could work well. If you like high-tech design, then you could want to make your office obviously functional: clients and customers can be reassured by the sight of office equipment, they see, literally, that you mean business. Sometimes, it can be easier to discipline oneself to work, if the home office is stark and highly functional in contrast with the rest of the house. On the other hand, you might want to maximise your use of space, by hiding away your office equipment in cupboards.

I should add a word about toilet facilities. It could spoil the business image for a caller to have to use a bathroom littered with children's plastic ducks or your damp bathrobe – strictly a part of private life. If there is no separate lavatory – make sure the bathroom is prepared for a meeting just as the office is.

YOUR 'CORPORATE' IMAGE

In the way that large companies create departments to deal with company image, if you are self-employed, starting your own business or are already in a small business, then you will need to consider image as an important issue. Your 'corporate' image needs to reflect the values of what you do and how the public reacts to your business, and these views need to be compatible. So if you open a bookshop and decide that it is a traditional, life-enhancing educational sort of business, your potential customers need to see these values echoed through your brochures, notepaper, advertising and packaging (design and copy); through the behaviour and dress of your staff, the decor and location of your premises and even, if you have one, the style of your delivery van.

In *Company Image and Reality* by David Bernstein, the author suggests that it is useful to see your business in terms of qualities that you would attribute to a person. This applies to service and product-based businesses; a training consultancy could be considerate, encouraging, innovative and productive; vitamin pills could be regarded as caring, informed, nourishing, energetic. Of course, you also need to consider who and where your market is, and how and when you will reach them. The reasons *why* your market should use your business should describe your company image. Perhaps you open a taxi company in a street full of restaurants and you appeal to customers because of the convenience factor. You might decide you want to reinforce this through your company image, publicising your service through the restaurants and calling your company Convenient Cabs.

Big companies often use slogans to encapsulate their corporate image – 'You can be sure of Shell', 'The listening bank' and 'We won't turn a drama into a crisis'. Respectively, these slogans convey qualities of reliability, accessibility and reassurance. They become synonymous with what we expect from these companies and help us to identify what they provide with our needs. The more a customer identifies his or her needs and values with a company, the more successful the business. We see particularly effective examples of this in companies with a distinctive 'philosophical' or 'lifestyle' image – the Body Shop, Conran, Laura Ashley and Next. The image of these companies and the values that they appeal to are exceptionally strong and clear.

Work Accessories

Whether you work for a large organisation or for yourself, the accessories that you use for work can say a lot about you. In the way that others notice your briefcase and watch, they will also notice your diary, folder, pen and desk accessories. Indeed, one of the most effective ways to personalise an office that has to be decorated and furnished in the same way as everyone else's is through choosing a colourful calendar or desk pad.

When you choose a good quality fountain pen and leather bound diary, you indicate to others a certain regard for quality and for tradition. Filofaxes are extremely popular and come in all shapes and sizes; it might be worth asking yourself whether a filofax is the most practical choice for you (some people may not need to carry an address and phone number section with them all the time; for the sort of work they do a large page-a-day desk diary would be a lot more practical) or whether you want to stand out from the crowd by choosing a different sort of diary.

If you visit clients and customers with proposals it may be worth investing in a smart stationery folder (Filofax make these). Your suggestions will then always look well-packaged.

Notepaper and Business Cards

Whether you are in business or not, your total image can be extended by developing a sense of how corporate image works. Many of us use headed notepaper and business cards, which send out signals that appeal to the logic and emotions of others. Once you have identified the 'personality' of your business you can use your choice of design, paper, typography and colour to reinforce your corporate image. In many cases, your headed notepaper can provide the first or an early introduction to your company, so the design is most important. If someone likes the look of your business card they are more likely to keep it and, hopefully, use it.

When choosing paper you can consider the texture, how rough or smooth it is and how light or heavy. If you are running a business with a 'glossy' image then you would be wise to reflect this in the type of paper you use; on the other hand, if your business provides a service that reassures others, you could opt to choose a rougher, light-absorbing, heavier paper that looks as though it has more depth. There are fashions in paper design, like everything else, and how fashionable you make your corporate image will depend on the business. It could be appropriate for an interior designer to use marbled paper, where an accountant using the same sort of paper could seem frivolous. You need to decide how much you want to indicate that your business is influenced by fashion and individual taste. The colours of business stationery are affected by fashions, too. Recently, a restrained and tasteful combination of grey and cream has been popular.

Type and paper colours suggest associations for recipients of your stationery. Some colours are more feminine than masculine; a haulage firm that used soft pink paper could be sending out a confusion of signals. If through your corporate image you wish to appeal more strongly to one sex than the other, then this criterion is important. Some combinations – dark brown lettering, or dark green on a cream background – look traditional, others, like black on white, look more distinctively business-like. If you use coloured paper it can change the colour of an ink that is used on it: a deep blue ink, for instance, can lose a lot of its 'blueness' when used on yellow paper. It is worth finding a helpful printer who can suggest whether certain combinations work well together.

If you decide that your business has a dynamic, energetic corporate image, then you could want to choose to have some yellow or red in the colour scheme. As a 'reassuring' business you could go for a conservative colour like navy blue or grey, and with an image that 'develops' and 'encourages personal growth' green could work well. Some colours, like peach and pink, can suggest luxury and indulgence. Indeed, a 'pampering', 'glamorous' corporate image can be suggested through stationery design that makes you feel as though you are giving yourself a treat just by looking at the card or notepaper.

Typefaces are powerful 'hidden persuaders' and need to be chosen with care. Type can represent corporate image when the company name is being reproduced in black and white. Some typefaces have been very popular for centuries; others are far more recent inventions. Choice of face can be influenced by how modern or traditional a corporate image you want to project; often, when companies pay a great deal of money to overhaul their image one of the major changes made is in typeface. When you choose a typeface, you can find out when it was created; and if you want to promote an 'elegant', 'stylish' corporate image you could go for a typeface which was designed in the 1920s or 1930s, a time when those qualities were foremost in design.

Readability is important, too, in the typeface you use; a very fancy one can be difficult to read and make poor initial impact. Typefaces with a lot of curvy lines will have a more feminine appeal that those with sharper, more geometric shapes. These guidelines also apply to a logo, which, if you choose to have one, should be simple, instantly recognisable and designed by a professional. If you are starting a business and cannot afford the services of a designer to help choose your typeface and paper, then look at the marketing of businesses similar to your own and work out what instincts in their customers they are trying to appeal to. Do they look as though they are being successful? Look at typefaces that you particularly like (those used by Chanel and Dunhill are typically distinctive, for instance) and consider whether they are appropriate for your corporate image. Capital letters can convey authority; small letters friendliness

Finally, and most important, the name you choose for your business should help its image. It can describe a product, a service or a major benefit and it should above all be memorable and concise. Spend time thinking about possible names and their appeal, and use dictionaries and friends for ideas. It is the name of your business, after all, that lets the public know who you are and invites them in.

Your Total Image has been written as an investigation into the signals we send out and how they are interpreted by others. The underlying theme that emerges is that we all have two conflicting needs; to connect with others and to express our individuality. I hope that this book has given you some ideas on how you interpret these two needs. I hope that it will help *you* to make the best of yourself.

For details of Philippa Davies' Successful Speaking course (1 day) and Presentation skills course (2 days), in-house company training, individual consultations and cassettes, please photostat and complete this form and send to VOICEWORKS, 223 HAMLET GARDENS, LONDON W6 0TS, or call 081–748 8318.

Name: _____

Address: _____

_____

I am interested in (please tick): public courses/in-house company training/individual consultation/cassettes.

READING LIST

Argyle, Michael *Bodily Communication* (Methuen)

   The Psychology of Interpersonal Behaviour (Penguin)

Berry, Ciceley *Your Voice and How to Use it Successfully* (Harrap)

Bixler, Susan *The Professional Image* (Perigee)

Braysich, Dr Joseph *Body Language* (Joseph Braysich, Australia)

Craig, Marianne *Office Workers' Survival Handbook* (BSSRS Publication)

Dunckel, J and Parnham, E *Business Guide to Effective Speaking* (Kogan Page)

Elsea, Janet *The Four Minute Sell* (Arrow)

Fast, Julius *Body Language* (Pan)

Faux, Susie with Philippa Davies *Wardrobe* (Piatkus)

Gelb, Michael *Body Learning* (Aurum)

Goffman, Erving *The Presentation of Self in Everyday Life* (Penguin)

Hodgkinson, Liz *The Alexander Technique* (Piatkus)

Honey, John *Does Accent Matter?* (Faber)

Jacques, Barbara *The Colour and Style File* (Piatkus)

King, Norman *The First Five Minutes* (Simon & Schuster)

Linehan, Dr Marsha and Egan, Dr Kelly *Asserting Yourself* (Century)

Mcallion, Michael *The Voice Book* (Faber)

Rowe, Dorothy *The Successful Self* (Fontana)

Skynner, Robin and Cleese, John *Families and How to Survive Them* (Methuen)

Tanner, Deborah *That's Not What I Meant* (Dent)

Turk, Christopher *Effective Speaking* (Spon)

Wells, Brian *Body and Personality* (Longman)

INDEX

Note: page numbers in italic refer to illustrations